20th Century Design:
A READER'S GUIDE

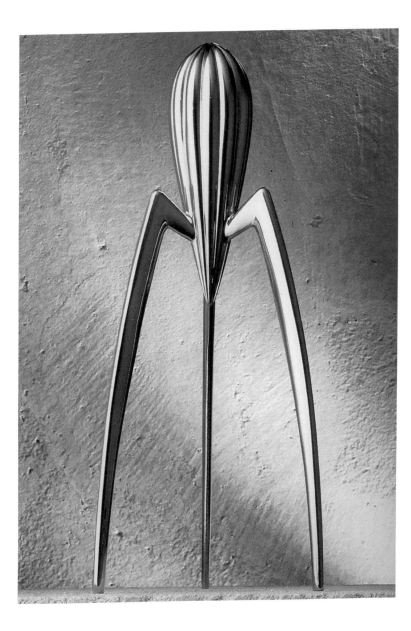

20th Century Design:
A READER'S GUIDE

Conway Lloyd Morgan

Architectural Press

OXFORD AUCKLAND BOSTON JOHANNESBURG MELBOURNE NEW DELHI

This book is for Annette, with love

Architectural Press
An imprint of Butterworth-Heinemann
Linacre House, Jordan Hill, Oxford OX2 8DP
225 Wildwood Avenue, Woburn, MA 01801-2041
A division of Reed Educational and Professional Publishing Ltd

A member of the Read Elsevier plc group
First published 2000

British Library Cataloguing in Publication Data
Morgan, Conway Lloyd
    20th Century Design: A Reader's Guide
    1. Design – History – 20th Century
    I. Title
    745.4'442
Library of Congress Cataloguing in Publication Data
A catalogue record for this book is available from the Library of Congress

ISBN 0 7506 4651 9

Printed and bound in Great Britain by Biddles Ltd
www.biddles.co.uk

Title page: Juicy Salif by Starck for Alessi
Overleaf: aerial photo of trenches near Metz

Contents

The Value of Enchantment

Aerial trench photograph, 1917

products of new mass-manufacturing systems. If design created itself out of the chaos of the post-1918 experience, it also carries as a birthmark the ambiguity inherent in trying to arbitrate the new, of trying to create aesthetic value for a new mercantile culture.

For some critics, notably Pevsner, this notion leads ineluctably back to the nineteenth century attitudes of Morris and the Arts and Crafts Movement. This is a false perspective, in my view. Morris and those around him were trying to refuse a process which, with some reason, they saw as harmful. Their attitude was one of denial. For twentieth century designers, whether idealists such as Walter Gropius or opportunists such as Raymond Loewy, the new order of things represented an immense opportunity to fashion the world anew. They rushed headlong into the embrace of industry, only finding out later what a fickle and changeable lover they had chosen. Design, like many other twentieth century cultural forms, such as theatre, literature and cinema, has a centre of self-awareness, a consciousness of its own existential ambivalence. And while it can be argued that modern theatre, art and literature have their origins in the period before the First World War, the notion of design in the contemporary sense of the word is wholly contemporary.

There are in one version of the story of early twentieth century design two broad main narratives, separated, it sometimes seems, by the Atlantic Ocean. One is the European story, starting with Le Corbusier, Marinetti, or Gropius, as your taste prefers. These pioneers set out to fashion ideologies that could be grafted onto industry: they sought to educate through example. The American story is of designers inventing a role for themselves within industry, as with Norman Bel Geddes and Raymond Loewy, and more concerned with giving form to new generations of products than with a thematic wider vision. This could be summarised as the Europeans making form follow function, and the Americans as using form to express function, a simplification that sidesteps the problem of finding a visual metaphor for a product with a new function, such as a radio. With the exodus of design talent from Europe to America at the end of the 1930s, and the influx of American products into Europe, either directly or through the media (particularly cinema), during and after the Second World War, these two streams mingle, creating a pop/Pop culture that Europe re-exported to America in the 1960s, and today to an international design culture that can find an American designing in Paris as easily as an Italian working in Tokyo or an Australian in Milan, and the same products on the shelves of shops all around the world.

The Second World War was the culmination of this design diaspora. And the War created new industries and industrial methods, and led to the creation of new towns, during the war in America and post-war in Europe, as well as economic and social demand for new household goods, cars and airplanes. This underlines the contention that the true driving force behind design since the War has been economics and technology as much as ideology. New materials and new manufacturing processes, especially in the field of electronics, have created new products for new markets, and new media, again primarily electronic, have created a galaxy of new visual expressions which in turn have fed into the creation of forms in product design. Design has thus become about mediating between a whole range of available visual languages, or families of imagery, as well as about the earlier task of expressing the function of a product through its form.

This is not a wholly new problem, though we tend to assume that the present visual glut offered by the new media is unprecedented. Take Harley Earl's Le Sabre car, designed according to the precepts of jet propulsion but built for roads restricted to a maximum of 55 miles per hour. The deliberate borrowing of imagery from fighter aircraft was, in Earl's case, an appeal to redneck machismo wholly devoid of irony. Or take Raymond Loewy's famous design for a streamlined pencil sharpener. It, too, is replete with anachronism – who expects to have to sharpen a pencil at Mach 1, and who needs pencils in the high-speed office, after all. The absurdity of the design – streamlining an immobile object – is tempered by visual effectiveness and self-awareness so as to create what could be called a quintessential object, an icon of the conflicts, ambiguities and subtleties of contemporary design. Forty to fifty years after these designs, Italian groups such as Memphis offered a selection of objects replete with deliberate irony, with rather more effect than the heavy wit of their contemporary colleagues in architecture, the post-Modernists.

This book sets out to look at twentieth century design through the cracked, or at least distorted, mirror of publications on design. The books presented in the following pages are not a canon of 'good design' or even good design writing, tempting as it might be, in millenarian mode, to set up such a gallery of false gods. Even less is this a 'designer's bookshelf' or some sort of ideal reading list. Rather it is an attempt to show how reading can be of interest or possibly benefit design, as well as showing how, occasionally, the printed word has been able to explain, interpret or preach for design ideas. This is above all a personal selection, based on twenty or so years of publishing and writing about, and occasionally taking part in, design.

Some of the reviews that appear here were written for publication, some are commentaries that I wrote for my own use, either to ensure, hopefully, that I had grasped what the author was on about, or to define more clearly an alternative to a particular publishing project. Some, perhaps the larger part, were specifically written for this book. In some cases I adopted the standpoint of an independent reviewer, in others I have tried to relate my comments to the wider themes of the functions of design and the designer in today's society. Some of the titles reviewed I personally had a hand in publishing. One of these is Marinetti's *Futurist Cookbook*, a book I had been fascinated by ever since finding mention of it in Elizabeth David's *Italian Food* some thirty years ago. Thanks to Susan Brill and Lutz Becker I was lucky enough to get the English language rights for it. Marinetti's book was a late 1930s classic: another from the same era was Le Corbusier's *Aircraft* which I also reprinted, as a facsimile (along with Loewy's *Aircraft*, both published by The Studio), and I also republished, though in a different format, Stephen Bayley's *Harley Earl*. Another book I published was the first edition of Sebastian Cater's *Twentieth-Century Type Designers*. But it was my colleague John Latimer Smith who created the project and saw it through publication, so I feel I can comment on it from a reasonable distance. Finally there is Martin Pawley's *Buckminster Fuller*. Asking Martin to write for me was the start of a lasting friendship and I hesitated for that reason over including his book. Two considerations decided me for inclusion: the fact that Martin is far too experienced an author to have taken any notice of any editorial interventions I might have made, and the fact that his book is the best one on Fuller, a major if quite obtuse figure in twentieth-century design.

I have chosen three principal categories of books. Firstly, works by designers themselves. From a literary point of view many of these prove that designers see better than they write, but such books do provide unique insights into the design process. Secondly there are books ostensibly about design, either by academics – including the newly-invented class of design historians – or by general writers. These often provide links to contemporary thinking, and alternative perspectives to the self-views of designers. And thirdly there are a number of specific books (and films) which are not directly about design but which, to my mind, have had an important influence on design or illustrate the world in which design operates or shows ways in which designers can benefit from a different viewpoint, or from the discipline of subjects at first sight wholly unrelated to design. I make no apologies for this third category, whose content is inevitably personal, and indeed provides the touches of colour in the Harlequin's coat of such a collection as this. And Harlequin's coat may look good on stage and tattered in daylight, something which echoes the changes in fashions of design as well.

For design is now wholly pervasive, at least in Western society. The perceived quality of consumer goods is often linked closely to the way in which they are advertised: slogans from advertising enter popular language: as Stephen Bayley has pointed out the word designer itself has now become an adjective, for describing jeans, aftershave, toothpaste or whatever (and so, he argues, losing any meaning, rather as terms such as 'executive' did some years earlier.) Objects by Alessi dot the wedding lists of the young middle classes, and the choice of furniture and decor makes or breaks the reputation of new restaurants and bars. This is the visible – some would say superficial – side of design: design as fashion. There is more serious ways in which design has extended its spread. The methodologies of design have been taken into wider aspects of business: no-one planning a new corporate identity campaign now stops at new logos and letterheads, but seeks to link the new image to a new consciousness (the 'mission statement'.) The expansion of the Internet and World Wide Web, the growth in terrestrial and satellite television have also accelerated the change from a word-based to an image-based world. These changes are increasing in pace, and the design profession is changing with them: interactive and website design has a key role, ending the traditional split between two- and three-dimensional design, and creating new obligations and demands on designers.

There is, despite this, a continuing tendency in design publishing to separate two- and three-dimensional design, and to concentrate on graphics. This is a reflection of market forces as much as anything, but it distorts the evolution of ideas and philosophies in design, and the longer-term interface between design and society that products, with their (relatively) longer presence creates. So I make no apology for putting into the same book graphics, product, furniture, deign management and design theory. There is a serious purpose to this harlequinade. As the European world moves away from product-based economies to service-based ones, as the media become more mediated, as public values erode in favour of private interests, the role of design in communications grows more important, and the need to understand and interpret the design process and the effect of design grows as well.

The French designer Philippe Starck has for several years been insisting on the duty of the designer to mobilise society into an awareness of its vulnerability and loss of options in a mutating environment. There are ambiguities in Starck's position, but his basic theme, one that in turn forms part of a tradition of demanding responsibility from design, is an increasingly valid one.

In a world dominated by the image, the entropy of ambiguity inevitably increases. Thus the importance of decrypting design also increases, for those of use who use design, and the responsibility of awareness on designers also becomes paramount. This awareness they can absorb from other media, from architecture, film, sociology, history and technology. Starck once said to me that 'designers should read about everything except design'. This dictum has never been far from my mind in composing this harlequinade.

Conway Lloyd Morgan
Chez le Pauvre, Le Vourdiat, 1999

In the Beginning

PAUL FUSSELL
THE GREAT WAR AND MODERN MEMORY
Oxford University Press, Oxford 1975

If we are to consider the twentieth century we should be-
gin at the beginning. The twentieth century began – or
rather the nineteenth century ended – not at midnight on
some December 31st, but in August 1914, with the start
of the First World War. Four and some years later, when
the war ended, the social, economic and political map of
Europe had been radically redrawn, with consequences for
the rest of the world. Those who like to see patterns in
history will no doubt recall that the war began after an
assassination in the Balkans, and that what England feared
in 1914 was not war in Europe but war in Ireland: 85
years on there is still wanton political murder in the Balkans and trouble in Ulster.

The First World War as a marker of violent social change,
of the ending of an established order, is a familiar trope.
What is not so familiar, but what is rather more important, is what replaced the established order: chaos, perhaps,
but chaos with perceptible forms and styles. Paul Fussell,
in his 1975 book *The Great War and Modern Memory*,
analyses the context of First World War English literature
as a mirror or result of this change. His analysis, in particular of the writings of Sassoon, Owen, Graves, Thomas,
Jones and Blunden, relates their personal experience to the
landscape of the war and looks at how this transmutes
into verse. The fact that on the Western Front the trench
lines ran north-south, for example, gave sunrise and sunset additional layers of meaning. From an English
standpoint, the sun rose over the enemy lines and set behind theirs. Add to this that dawn and dusk were considered

to be the favourite moments for an enemy attack, times at which all ranks 'stood to', that is, took up their firing positions in the trenches and observed the enemy lines, as best they could, and the normal poetic connotations of the sun's movement in the heavens are at once extended. And as Fussell points out, the use of poetic or rhetorical diction was a way of talking about the war: the dead were 'the fallen', soldiers are 'warriors', sleep 'slumber,' danger 'peril', and so on. Before any ideas of the grim realities of modern warfare could even emerge, they had to break through this mock chivalric curtain of language, and then find a language capable of expressing the actual, everyday horrors of life at the Front. This task was near impossible: David Jones retreated into myth, Robert Graves into theatre, Siegfried Sassoon into parody – the latter taking thirty years to achieve.

Besides formal literary writing there were the myths that grew or were invented around the fighting. Some of these, such as the Angel of Mons, appear to have been deliberately developed or exploited as pieces of propaganda, defined by E.M. Cornford as 'the art of completely confusing one's friends without quite deceiving one's enemies'. Other myths seem more spontaneous – the Corpse Rendering Factory, for example, or the army of deserters that lived underground in no-man's-land, black jokes invented by the lost in a dark landscape. But the greatest barrier of myth (and of experience) was the one that lay between the soldiers at the front and those at home. Journalists kept well away from the trenches (as did the General Staff) and what was revealed about the actual conditions of fighting was strictly censored. There was news about the war, couched in a language that made it seem as if great events were unfolding according to order and pattern, rather than the haphazard struggle in mud for metres of trench that was the actuality. That military terminology entered everyday English and has remained there, reinforced by the proliferation of war in the twentieth century. Business in particular has picked up on this vocabulary: market forces, takeover battles, product positions, all are, Fussell suggests, part of an unconscious legacy from the Great War. But the myths were more important than these in-formal borrowings. Or rather, what happened to the myths, and the deceptions they concealed, for a time. It was the extent of that deception, when revealed by the end of the war, as well as the sense of pointless and futile loss, that broke the social order. Truth, and innocence, were the first casualties of the fighting. They were replaced by absurdi-ty and irony. Nothing could be taken on trust again. In Fussell's words 'I am saying that there seems to be one dominating form of modern understanding: that it is es-sentially ironic: and that it originates largely in the appli-cation of mind and memory to the events of the Great War'. Fussell understands irony as the only response of the impotent, the character hounded by absurdity and power-less to stop it.

What Fussell says about literary understanding can I think be applied equally to our understanding of architecture, design and art. In the twentieth century we have not mere-ly seen the ending of established orders (in the way that Gothic architecture gave way to Classical models in the Renaissance, for example.) We have lost the idea of order altogether: there are no appeals to precedent today. We have not arrived at this position through the direct trau-ma of the Great War, nor of the subsequent wars of the century. But our awareness of the reality of war, its ca-pacity for horror, its pointlessness and seeming necessity – itself an immense irony – has shaped our memory and so our culture. This knowledge makes us feel on the one hand powerless, in the sense of irony developed by Northrop Frye in his analysis of modes of fiction. (Frye suggests fic-tion can be categorised according to the freedom of actions of the hero compared with the ordinary man: if it larger, then fiction can be likened to myth, if it is the same, to comedy or melodrama, but where the hero is less power-ful, then the mode of fiction is ironic.) But on the other hand liberation from the canons of the past or the constraints of example is itself of value, even in an impotent situation. We are freed as well to discover for ourselves, even if our knowledge suggests this freedom is circumscribed. This dichotomy between restraint and opportunity can be seen as a creative force, infusing the everyday with new layers of meaning, and creating opportunities for new definitions, new formulations and new expressions. This sense of awareness, of our accidental and fragile existence on a minor planet in a small galaxy, is also one of the aspects that makes the twentieth century's sense of culture and experience different from those of the past, and why we can therefore talk of design as a specifically twentieth century activity. If the First World War has orphaned us from optimism, it has also created, for the aware, a potential and a need for new means of expression. Design is one of these.

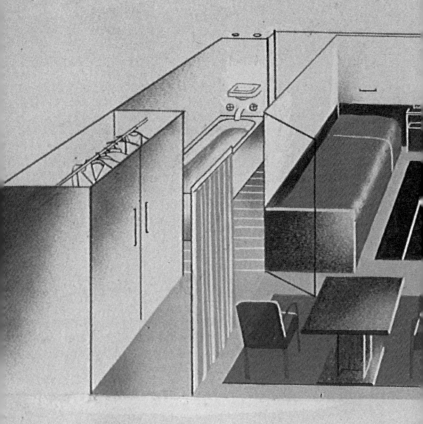

Design for a steamship cabin by Brian O'Rourke

Serious Europe

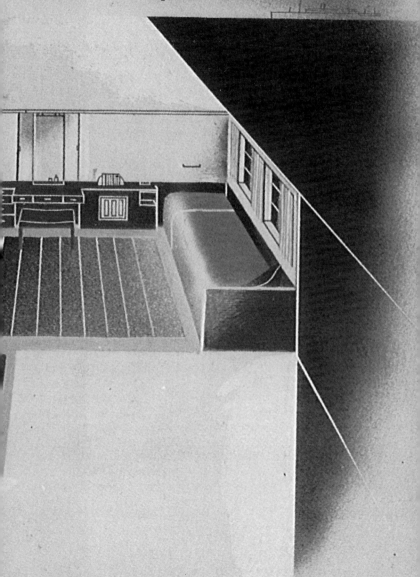

Making by Doing

DAVID PYE
THE NATURE OF DESIGN
Studio Vista, London, 1970

One afternoon in the mid-1960s, an editor realised that a photograph of Rodin's sculpture *The Kiss* needed for a book going to the printers the next day was not to hand. Phone calls to agencies and the Rodin Museum could not produce an immediate replacement. Such panics are not uncommon, but the solution found was unusual. The next morning the editor found what seemed to be a photograph of the sculpture on the desk: it transpired that two members of staff had taken up the pose and been photographed by a colleague! The publishing house that was such a hive of initiative was Studio Vista. The imprint, that had originally belonged to the Studio magazine, came into new ownership in the 1960s, with David Herbert as the editorial director. He set about producing a series of illustrated books that would introduce contemporary ideas in art, architecture and design to a new public.

The books were to be integrated (that is, illustrations and text were to be printed together, not split into different sections), with contemporary layout and typography, mainly using sans-serif faces and asymmetric typography, and sold in paperback at economical prices. John Lewis was the series editor for books on design: their distinctive square format has had an enduring impact on design publishing ever since. (As a technical solution it caused problems, since, as John Lewis later explained in an interview, to work economically two books had to be printed together, and two were never ready to the same time!) The range of authors recruited by the imprint is impressive: Peter Cook and Theo Crosby on architecture, Paul Rand, Colin Forbes and Alan Fletcher on graphics, Aaron Scharf on photograhy, and David Pye on the nature of design.

David Pye starts from the position that we cannot decide what constitutes good design before we have a clear idea of what design is. His definition is based on the evolution of forms from the demands of function, drawing from the history of technology traditional devices such as adzes and anchors, up to contemporary aircraft (in this case the ill-fated British TSR2 strike jet). This leads him to modernist definition of the values of the utilitarian: 'the only work which is entirely useless is the doing of redundant operations or the adding of redundant components, such as applied ornaments'. He argues from the principles of mechanical engineering that any designed object needs to balance requirements of economy, energy and use in addition to the preferences of the designer.

Every design is an approximation, a compromise, limited by our available knowledge and resources, and that a 'finished' design is not a solution, but only a possible solution waiting to be tested. 'At one time a flake of flint was fit for the purpose of surgery, and stainless steel is not fit for the purpose yet. Every thing we design is an improvisation, a lash-up, something inept and provisional. We live like castaways... But one day the dictionary may read Function: What someone has provisionally deduced that a device may reasonably be expected to do at present'. Pye is ably aware of the anomalies of the formal Modernist argument, and the imprecision with which 'function' has so often been defined. His book is a valuable, elegant and above all rational analysis of the form/function debate, and rests its case on tradition and physics as much as on ideology.

Aligning the Argument

Nikolaus Pevsner
PIONEERS OF MODERN DESIGN
From William Morris to Walter Gropius
Penguin Books, Harmondsworth, 1985
(First edition 1936)

Pevsner's thesis is a straightforward one: that there is a direct line linking the nineteenth century reformers such as Morris and Ruskin to the Modern Movement as espoused and expounded by Gropius and the Bauhaus, and that this line is the one true path for the design and architecture of the twentieth century. 'Morris laid the foundations of the modern style: with Gropius its character was ultimately determined', he writes. The linking factor is the social role of artistic activity, exemplified by Morris's refusal to dissociate art from morality, politics or religion, and modified by Gropius's discovery of the power for good of the machine. Progress, social, technical and material, is the artist's sacred duty. Leaving the true path is an abomination – Gaudi and Sant'Elia's works, which do not, mercifully, fit the straitjacket of the author's ordered thinking, were consigned in the first editions to the footnotes : they are now in, qualified as 'fantastical rantings'.

Pevsner's arguments against gratuitous decoration and inappropriate forms are vigorous and uncompromising. The same magisterial style made his *Outline History of European Architecture* a student bible and his *High Victorian Design* a book of revelations. Pevsner, who emigrated from Germany to Britain in 1933, dying in London in 1988, exercised an immense effect on architectural and art history in Britain. From its first publication in 1936, under the telling title in the USA of *Pioneers of the Modern Movement*, this book influenced the thinking of generations of students, inspiring or dragooning them to seek purpose behind form, to disdain decoration and to eschew enjoyment. We can now look at his writing with over half a century of hindsight, and not be so tempted into the mechanics of the Modern Movement argument, but the book's stranglehold on an epoch is not lightly overlooked. The thesis proposed, the lamp of genius passed from hand to hand to the glorious moment of the Modern Movement, is at best simplistic, if not untenable: 'that peculiar and short-lived Expressionism in .... architecture which for a while held up the main stream of modern architecture' is a typical aside.

Pevsner's method comes from classical art history, which traced styles techniques and subjects from artist to artist across generations. It is an approach which, used sensibly, has its value in dealing with formal issues. As a device for connoisseurship it can be taken to extremes: I recall a museum curator asserting to me that a particular Dutch 17th century painting used a composition taken from an early 16th century Italian original even though the Dutch artist had never travelled to Italy nor had the Italian work been engraved! And the fact that an artist borrowed an idea from Raphael does not mean that he painted like Raphael, even less that he thought like him. So to apply this technique to validate a history of ideas is in fact a *post hoc, propter hoc* fallacy. Priority does not validate posterity, and there is no inevitable logic or progression that ensure inevitable rightness of modernism.

Pevsner's training as an art historian led him to identify individuals as sole makers, and to assume that their work was, like an artist's, simply the direct expression of his or her ideas and ideals (contemporary art history now places much more reliance on factors such as patronage, the social position of artists and the role of the art market). As such, his analysis of individual works and buildings – much of the book deals with architecture rather than design as such – is often stimulating and always acute. But the needs of his thesis lead him at times even to dehumanize his heroes: there is a telling aside on Corbusier's church at

Ronchamp, which Pevsner has to see as a throwback to the Sagrada Familia, rather than accepting that Corbusier's vision was larger. But Pevsner's starting point ignores the social context, and it ignores teamwork, which is in fact the essence of actual architectural and design practice today.

Concepts such as client, context, cost and planning hardly appear at all: manufacturers are pushed aside as 'uneducated' in the nineteenth century, and their role with designers later not mentioned at all (so leaving out, as superfluous to the argument, AEG and Peter Behrens in Germany, or Jack Beddinton at Shell in Britain). Pevsner's intellectual construct is impressive, but a folly as well. The book proposes a single-track historical vision that may have been relevant for the post-Versailles Germany where it was first formulated, and its tenacity on foreign soil is proof of the intellectual power of that epoch – but not of the book's relevance to a contemporary audience. Design is not a relay-race of heroes, but something more complex, more involved with technology, culture and society, and more interesting than that.

Flying to the Future

LE CORBUSIER
AIRCRAFT
The Studio, London 1935

'The airplane is the symbol of the new age' declares Le Corbusier in the preface to this montage of images and texts, first published by the *Studio* in 1935. Gliders and seaplanes, contrails, aerobatics and aerial photographs, wheel struts, propellers, tieframes and cylinder blocks are accompanied by hortatory texts enthusing over the expansion of the world offered by flight, the contemporary forms of the machine, the new architecture of the skies. Images of an aircraft carrier are entitled 'and Neptune rises from the sea, crowned with strange garlands, the weapons of Mars'.

Corbusier's bibliography is rather longer than his list of built work. This is true of many architects, and is not meant negatively. In Corbusier's case it is best seen as part of the general programme he set himself, to spread the cause of the new architecture in as many ways as he could, through writing, publications, painting and building. This polyvalent approach is typical of the interwar years, when others – even if of different persuasions, such as Marinetti – saw themselves as Renaissance creatures, able to put their skills and ideas into any field.

For Corbusier, the aircraft here is used to represent the formal and functional values of modernism. The new form becomes a platform for attacking older views 'The only monotony is created by the Academies. Life is multiform'. The reductive process essential in aeronautical engineering, and the range of new forms that were explored in the immense development of aircraft design in the 1920s and 1930s, with the change from wooden biplanes to metal monoplanes, and the expansion of passenger travel (often through seaplanes) provided a rich gallery of pictures for Corbusier's comments. 'The airplane embodies the purest expression of human scale and a miraculous exploitation of material'.

From the records in the Corbusier Foundation in Paris, it would seem that the book was put together in London, apart from the main introductory text. There is no original French manuscript for the caption texts, and they have the sound of rapid translations. 'Once in the air, carried along by the wind, they exult in the daring of their departure'. This sort of phraseology, which one instinctively feels one sound better in French than in English, if anything adds to the immediacy and appeal of the book, a quality emphasised by the bold typography and bled images.

The final section of the book turns to the bird's eye view, and what this does to our perception of the world. 'The eye now sees in substance what the mind formerly could only subjectively conceive.... Man will make use of it to conceive new aims. New cities will arise out of their ashes'. There are profound ironies in this appeal for a new urbanism, given the destruction of cities from the air over the following decade. This in fact created the opportunities for the Modernists to put their ideas into practice. And, a final irony, the German bombing of London in 1942 destroyed the offices and warehouse of the *Studio*, together with any remaining stock of *Aircraft*.

Using the Technology

TOLMER
MISE EN PAGE
The Studio, London, 1937

One Studio book not destroyed in the bombing of London
in 1942 was Tolmer's *Mise en Page*. It had been published
in 1937, in an edition of 1,500 copies, priced at five pounds
a copy (about two hundred pounds or three hundred dollars today). The production costs had been enormous and
unexpected, and staff at the *Studio*, still owned at the time
by the Holme family, were dubious about the likely sales,
particularly given the high price. In fact the book sold out
in three months, but was never reprinted: it is a graphic
bibliophile's grail to even see a copy today.

Tolmer was an advertising agent and designer based in Paris, and his book is a powerful argument for the creative
use of typography and design. He illustrates this with contemporary book and advertising design, as well as through
contemporary art. The case is also made through the typography and layout of the book itself. Much of what he
had to say in the 1930s appears conventional today, and
much of it had been said by the innovative typesetters of
the Bauhaus. But Tolmer, as both a practitioner and the-
oretician, validated the new approach for commercial type
design as well (though apart from some articles in the Studio magazine, I know of no other writing by him). Using
type for emphasis, varying fonts and weights, running type
around cut-out illustrations, in short seeing text, type and
images as a necessary whole, were at the core of his a-
genda. To understand how new and surprising this must
have seemed in England, we need to remember the emphasis on good taste and traditional type practice preached at
the time (and at *The Times*) by established figures such
as Stanley Morison and Oliver Simon. Morison led a clean-

up campaign to bring type design back to its original values, away from the clutter accumulated in the nineteenth
century, and to encourage the design of new types in the
true spirit of Renaissance typography, while the private
press movement, of which Simon was a leading member,
sought to ally modernity and taste through typographical-
ly transparent publications in limited editions.

The high production costs of the book were due to the additional pages interspersed into the book showing the latest
print technologies, such as printing on celluloid, printing
on flock wallpapers, cut-outs and pop-ups, printing using
special inks (including a fluorescent) and in techniques such
as rotogravure. While some of the images appear slightly
crude, it is worth remembering that printing on plastic, for
example, other than by silk-screen, was not available for
some thirty years after *Mise en Page* was published, and
that only in the last decade or so has printing on tracing
paper been feasible in colour at economical press speeds.
While little is known about the author, there would seem
to be hardly any doubt that Tolmer designed these pages
himself, and they are a large part of what makes the book
so special (and rare). Tolmer's willingness to demonstrate
the potential of new technologies makes the book all the
more remarkable, in that it encompasses so many of the
ideas about typography that we now see as part of a much
later revolution, but which were put down on paper fifty
years before the Apple Mac hit the design studio.

Learning through Longing

ADRIAN FORTY
OBJECTS OF DESIRE
Thames & Hudson, London 1986

The author's intention is simple: to link the development of household equipment to the story of industry in the period 1750-1980, and survey the social changes brought about by the mechanisation of the home and the mass production of housewares, such ascrockery and cookware. Adrian Forty's *Objects of Desire* was written in 1980 and published a few years after. Forty's subject is the design manufacturing and social status of household goods in the period from 1750 to 1980. The first part of the book concerns Josiah Wedgwood's innovative role in the pottery business, and in particular his reorganisation of a craft workforce into a structured factory system, and the role of the modellers employed to create deigns for serial production.

For Forty, Wedgwood's humble and anonymous modellers are themselves the model for the true role of the designer for the next two and a quarter centuries. This process of masking the individuality of the designer allows him to focus on the one hand on the importance of the manufacturer's role as a decision maker, in terms of which designs reached the marketplace – for example he cites the nineteenth century cotton makers who would purchase 2,000 designs but only ever print 500 on their new steam presses – and the social tendencies, particularly in regard to the respective notions of class, women, housework and home, that also influenced the actual marketplace for designed goods.

For 1980, Forty's standpoint was a new and dynamic one. His treatment of that Wedgwood, for example, runs completely counter to other accounts of the changes in pottery design, from the same period, which blindly assumed some force such as taste was driving the changes in patter, colour and imagery. Wedgwood emerges from Forty's account as a true entrepreneur a position justified by his citations of Wedgwood's own correspondence with Thomas Bentley, his London agent and in some way his mentor in taste. Similarly his account of the moral definition of the Victorian bourgeois home and the pressures that created on wives also put the excess of Victorian design into a new context.

Coming to the twentieth century Forty is strong on dealing with the redefinition of housework in the absence of a servant class, and on the efforts of manufacturers to sell new technologies, especially electricity, wireless and refrigeration. Again, manufacturing visions and social effects underline his arguments. He is particularly interesting on the ways in which manufacturers tried to contextualize new products, such as radios, either by disguising them as old forms of furniture (the 'radio cabinet') or by burying them inside existing pieces (the radio armchair is a particular delight) or by trying to find new forms in new and so modern materials such as Bakelite. He also gives a detailed account of one of the most important English corporate identity programmes of the interwar years, the creation of a new and modern image for London Transport in the hands of the general manager, Frank Pick, who used the amalgamation of previous independent services into a new single whole as an opportunity to foster modern typography and modern architecture in the new entity. For Forty, as for many writers, Frank Pick is seen as a model of the enlightened manager.

As a corollary of his insistence on the role of managers and of social constraints in the design process, Forty also argues against histories of design or presentations of design ideas that are based on the personalities and lives of designers. As he points, this is a model derived from Pevsner's *Pioneers of Modern Design*, in which the transmission of the concept of Modernism from pioneer to pioneer was an essential part of his ideological argument. It was also a model borrowed in its turn from art history and connoisseurship. By ignoring context it is an inadequate model (though as Forty admits, Giedion's social forces only model also begs as many questions as it seeks to answer).

But the portrayal of design as being led by entrepreneurs not by designers begins to unravel in the face of actual twentieth century practice, which suggests that the continuity that Forty claims between 18th and nineteenth century modes of designing the contemporary ones has in fact broken, in the light of changing social and economic patterns and the increased perception of the role of design. Forty cites the redesign of the Lucky Strike cigarette packet by Raymond Loewy as an example of design that has been used by its designer to promote his self-notion of omnipotence. Loewy certainly put the word I into designer, and saw self-promotion as a sacred duty, but even so Forty's account misses the point. He starts by claiming that American Tobacco, the makers of Lucky Strike, has decided on a redesign 'for reasons that are not known'. Loewy simplified the design, losing the background green in favour of white and repeating the main logo on both sides to double visibility.

Forty argues that anyone could have made these changes, and that their success (the pack has scarcely been touched since) was due to the design embodying, at the time, a vision of cleanliness and quality that was specifically American, and so turning the brand into a specifically American statement. Loewy's own account of the matter is much more flamboyant: the head of American Tobacco breezes into Loewy's office unannounced one morning, and challenges him to do something with the design that will increase sales. Loewy takes up the challenge, making a bet out of it that his design can increase sales. The redesign work drops the green (the ink smelt odd anyway) and by resetting the typematter on a solid red disc strengthens the impact of the name. Loewy himself points out that the whiteness gave a 'clean and impeccable' look to the product. What is interesting in Loewy's account is that it shows

American Tobacco realising that the new breed of independent design consultants that had emerged in the wake of the Depression could deliver something through design that the manufacturers could not achieve themselves (if, as Forty suggests, anyone could have done the redesign, why did they not do it themselves?) Loewy also intuited, correctly, that a cleaner pack would look more American, and so do better. And Loewy did take manufacturing concerns into account (losing the green ink saved money). The Lucky Strike pack is a key example of a new relationship between designer and manufacturer emerging, which broke with the previous convention of the manufacturer as omnipotent (not that this new deal granted omnipotence to the designer either).

Forty's model of design as designers submitting a series of preliminary sketches from which the manufacturer chooses and implements what suits him may have been true in the past, but the contemporary mature practice of design is wholly different: the work of modern design companies runs into levels of research and analysis for their clients that carry the designer into the heart of the production process, in a continuous exchange of information and opinion. Granted, this often involves designers in understanding and adopting the ideological stance of their clients, and so participating in the capitalist system. But designers have achieved their current role by bringing more than acquiescence to the table. Companies all over the world have recognised the value of design not merely in selling products and services, but in creating an economic order in which the values and views of consumers are also represented, in which companies address, at least to some extent, social issues about pollution and resources and about business ethics. That designers and, even more so, their clients could do more in this respect, is not in doubt. But to equate contemporary designers with Wedgwood's humble modellers is not merely an inaccuracy but a disservice to the profession of design.

Serving up Mussolini

F.T. MARINETTI
THE FUTURIST COOKBOOK
Translated by Sue Brill with an introduction by Leslie Chamberlain
Trefoil, London 1989

History has not been kind to the Italian Futurists, leaving them as a dangling marginal note to the grand sweep of Modernism, or passing them by as a freak moment in time, when it so happened that a few young men were rich enough to own their own cars and clever enough, nearly, to drive them – a reference to the passionate description of an automobile accident that prefaced one of the group's many manifestoes. But what the Futurists claimed, or rather proclaimed, was, like the Modernists, the dawn of a new era, in which the machine – in the form of the car and the aeroplane – would be the dominant symbol, and speed and movement the only metaphors. And in the light of this new vision they set out to reorganise the world: new art and new literature, new typography, new clothes, new buildings – and new food. Other movements, such as the Russian Constructivists, and individuals such as Le Corbusier and Buckminster Fuller, had equally grand dreams which they unrolled before the world through texts, exhortations and examples. So why have the Futurists been ignored for so long?

The answer has to do with the nature of the group itself, and the character of its leading figure, Marinetti. The history of Italian Futurism falls into two sections, one preceding and during the first world war, the other from the 1920s onwards. In the first period the movement involved a number of artists, notably Boccioni, who either died during the war or left the group after it. The later recruits, in the second period, were not of the same calibre. And in the second period the Futurists aligned themselves with Mussolini's Fascists, taking up the same nationalistic and right-wing causes. This had two consequences: most other modernist groups were generally left-wing, as were most later commentators, and so what the Futurists had to say was suspect in itself, while within Italy after the defeat of Mussolini no-one wanted to mention the Futurists for several decades. The publishing history of the *Futurist Cookbook* is a case in point. Elisabeth David included a number of recipes from it in her *Italian Food*, and during the 1960s and early 1970s a number of publishers tried to obtain the rights to the complete volume. But the co-holders of the copyright would not hear of it, and publication had to wait until the expiry of one holder's rights. Since the main argument of the book is that excessive consumption of pasta is holding back the Italian people from their manifest destiny as a world power under their great leader Benito Mussolini, one can understand their reluctance.

One influence of the Futurist cookbook, despite its unavailability, can perhaps be seen in the virtues of presentation espoused by the *nouvelle cuisine* of the 1980s, a movement that arose contemporaneously with a major Futurist exhibition and banquet in Venice. For Marinetti's recipes were not just food statements, but visual concerts, often with deliberate puns and contrasts. For example, take the Aerosculptural Dinner in the Cockpit: 'in the large cockpit of a Trimotor, surrounded by metal aerosculptures by the Futurist Mino Rosso and Thayaht the diners will prepare a pasted of potato flour, little onions, eggs, prawns, pieces of sole, tomato and lobster meat, sponge cake and chopped biscuits, castor sugar with vanilla, candied fruits and gruyère cheese, soaked in plenty of Tuscan Vin Santo.

With this they fill eleven moulds (buttered and floured), each one in a shape typical of a mountain, a gorge, a promontory or small island. They will all be cooked electrically.

The eleven pies, removed from their moulds, will be served on a huge tray in the centre of the cockpit, while the diners toss in the air and devour masses of fluffy whipped egg white just as the wind outside plays with the white cirrus and cumulus clouds'.

Or another: Aerofood
'The diner is served from right with a plate containing some black olives, fennel hearts and kumquats. From the left he is served with a rectangle made of sandpaper, silk and velvet. The foods must be carried directly to the mouth with right hand while the left hand likely and repeatedly strokes the tactile rectangle. In the meantime the waiters spray the napes of the diners' necks with a conprofumo of carnations, while from the kitchen comes contemporaneously a violent conrumore of an aeroplane motor and some *dismusica* by Bach'.

Recipes such as these would not be found amiss at any later art happening or event. But what distinguished Marinetti's approach was his political stance. Obloquy and indifference are not the only reasons for the Futurists' obscurity. Filippo Tommaso Marinetti not only wrote and published the first *Futurist Manifesto*, published in *Le Monde* in February 1909, but he suggested, implemented, stage-managed and presented virtually every other Futurist event thereafter. The dynamics of the movement were not those of a group, but of a leader and his disciples. In Marinetti's case his passionate addiction to the virtues of warfare, his apparent xenophobia, and his early espousal of Fascism make him an unappealing character, as he stares truculently out from contemporary photographs, often dressed in flamboyant military uniform.

Food and Fun

ELIZABETH DAVID
A BOOK OF MEDITERRANEAN FOOD
Hamish Hamilton, London, 1950

Gertrude Stein recorded in her diary just after the liberation of Paris that, to mark the glad event, one of the art
dealers had put a marvellous canvas of a roast chicken in
his window. 'No-one had seen a roast chicken for years.'
she noted, thinking it a wonderful and subtle gesture. England had to wait a bit longer for the same gesture: it appeared in the form of Elizabeth David's 1950 title *A Book
of Mediterranean Food*. After years of rationing, Woolton
pie and tinned snoek, a fish that even the Oxford English
Dictionary refuses to admit exists, it was a breath of fresh
air, an offer of the possibility of authenticity and pleasure
from cooking. David's insistence on quality ('use good olive oil' at a time when olive oil was a bright yellow liq-
uid, slightly less viscous than water and available only from
chemists), and her sense of assurance reminded many people of what the pleasures of the table had been before the
war, and introduced a new world to others (including this
writer). But she did not only make recipes available, she
showed that cooking and entertaining were cultural activities. Her prose was well-written, firm and decisive, quite
unlike anything that might have been termed 'cookery writing' before.

The personality that seems to emerge from her pages is of
a rather restrained and formal figure, with a certain sense
of humour but a bit bossy. A recent biography by Artemis
Cooper shows this is only part of the story. Elizabeth David was certainly imperious, but hardly restrained: she spent
the first years of the war travelling round the Mediterranean with her lover, before ending up in Alexandria and
Cairo, then cities of intrigue and excess, as other writers

such as Laurence Durrell and Olivia Manning have shown. Norman Douglas was one of her mentors ('always do as you please and send everybody to hell and take the consequences' was one of the maxims he taught her, along with insisting on the best and refusing the bogus and second-rate).

Though she later wrote as enthusiastically about Italian and French cooking, it is appropriate that David's first book centred on the Mediterranean. As Paul Fussell has pointed out in his book *Abroad*, travel especially to the Mediterranean coast became a particular form of literary solace after the First World War; so it is apt that David should reintroduce the concept of pleasure into English cooking through a similar journey.

If circumstances of war brought Elizabeth David her chance of fame, she used it well. Her approach of explaining rather than dictating, her evident pleasure in sharing knowledge, inspired a complete change in writing about food, and the rise in quality in British cuisine since the war can be ascribed in part to her example. She was part of a wider movement in British life towards pleasure and away from the puritan values of the war years. Together with the designer Terence Conran, who created Habitat, and, a few years later, fashion icons such as Biba and Mary Quant, David taught the English that they could enjoy themselves: as she herself said 'people must make their own discoveries, use their own intelligence, otherwise they will be deprived of part of the fun'.

Modernising the Century

JEREMY AYNSLEY
NATIONALISM AND INTERNATIONALISM
SUSAN LAMBERT
FORM FOLLOWS FUNCTION ?
Design in the twentieth century series
Victoria and Albert Museum, London, 1993

Museums used to the places where we went as much to
pose questions as find answers. Now that the emphasis is
on the 'guest experience' in EuroDisney's ambiguous phrase,
the real is at risk of being lost behind the reconstructions.
The Victoria and Albert Museum in London has, hopefully, a sufficient density of collections, and sufficient acuity
in its curatorial staff, to evade this descent to the lowest
common denominator of instant response. These strengths
are shown in the museum's new gallery of twentieth century design, which houses both industrial and artisan products, graphics, textiles and furniture of the last 100 years.

The purpose behind the gallery is not only to present design objects in chronologically coherent groups but also to
introduce approaches to the design process, and suggest
how designers have gone about their work in different
ways. The two books under review are the first in a series
of seven, and continuing the theme of the gallery by looking at different aspects of designing. They are aimed at a
sixth-form and first year college market.

Aynsley's book is divided into two main sections, on in-
ternationalism and nationalism, each dealing with a number of different approaches to the concept, with a closing
section on regionalism and globalism. This plan is further
restricted by his taking a long run-up at these subjects. As

a result, many of the points he makes have no room for development or explanation.

It is a pity that the last section of the book, dealing with recent aspects of design, is the most compressed. The earlier sections, particularly those on design in Italy and Germany, are much stronger, and define well the author's notion of design as a cultural construct, reacting in relative ways to political and social circumstances and changes, but also informed by an internal discipline.

The second book in the series looks at one such discipline, form. Anyone familiar with Susan Lambert's earlier books on the function of drawing and on the transmission of works of art from prints will not the surprised at the breadth of learning and vision in her *Form Follows Function?*. Here she traces the development of the functionalist notion, and related ideas on truth to materials and pure forms, from Vitruvius up to the present. After a historical introduction, and a chapter, not surprisingly, on the Bauhaus, different aspects of the theme are presented in chapters on form and process, form and the design system, and form and identity.

Starting with Vitruvius is also taking a long view of the twentieth century; but the author here handles the transition less abruptly, and has a genial knack for finding unfamiliar but apt quotations to enliven and support the argument. This is that a formal analysis can be applied to the design process at different stages and in different ways, and can still be a valid approach to design despite the collapse of a narrow definition of form after Modernism. The broad texture of this argument allows for a good range of examples to be brought in, but again the strength of the approach falters when dealing with current products. But as a review of design in the earlier part of this century the text is excellent, and has the advantage that much of the work here discussed is publicly accessible.

Practical America

Future Spaces

HUGH FERRISS

THE METROPOLIS OF TOMORROW

Princeton Architectural Press, New York, 1986
(reprint)

Our perceptions of the city are modelled by a range of images: films, books, posters, news stories. But if there is an
ur-image of the American city, it must be in Hugh Ferriss's
work. From 1915 to the 1950s he worked as a professional
architectural illustrator, preparing renderings for many major New York firms, the doyen of his profession. Early on,
in 1925 he had an exhibition of visionary drawings at the
Anderesen Gallery in New York, and in 1929 he published
the first edition of this book. This had an immediate impact
on the architectural public, and was extremely influential in
film set design (David Butler's sci-fi *Just Imagine* of 1930,
for example). In 1939 Ferriss worked with Norman Bel Geddes on the Futurama at the New York Worlds Fair, one of
the most visionary and popular exhibits.

The book is in three sections: a first set of actual projects
from around the USA: the St. Louis telephone building, the
Chrysler building in New York (then still under construction), the Los Angeles City Hall, and others. This section
introduces Ferriss's drawing style: monochrome renderings
in charcoal, with strong and dramatic lighting effects. Perspectives are normally taken from ground level, and
foreshortened to increase the grandeur of the skyscrapers.
The second section looks at projected trends. Here Ferriss
drew on his work with the NY City Commissioners on zon-
ing in urban planning, and in designing step-back skyscrapers
that would admit more light to street level. He argues strongly for planned development, to avoid overcrowding the urban
landscape. In the urban fabric, he envisages pedestrian walk-
ways above car-filled streets, glass-fronted skyscrapers, and

twentieth-floor hangars for personal aircraft. The third section takes the trends for individual buildings to create An Imaginary Metropolis. This is divided into three zones – Business, Art, Science – each dominated by a huge central building, and surrounded by lower buildings for housing and services, and linked by master highways. The three centres are pivotal both to the design and the functioning of the city, even to its government. They are placed equidistant from each other on the radius of the central circle of the city, with their relative sectors radiating out behind them, and related building along the chord – so that the Applied and Industrial Arts building is between the Art and Business centres, for example.

Ferriss's attempt to create a city 'populated by human beings who value emotion and mind equally with the senses' is, with hindsight, wholly idealised, and far from the reality of modern urban chaos. But if the arguments are idealistic, the force of his imagery, and his identification of coming ideas, have made this book a highly influential document.

Princeton Architectural Press (which in the best tradition of such names is of course now based in New York) began by issuing excellent facsimile reprints of classical architectural texts such as Ledoux's *L'Architecture*, and have then moved into general architecture and design publishing. Their books are distinguished by their excellent production values, typography and design, and are a happy proof that a small but committed publisher can prosper even in the current age of conglomerates.

Design by Slogan

RAYMOND LOEWY
NEVER LEAVE WELL ENOUGH ALONE
Simon & Schuster, New York, 1955

'Loewy with his Coke bottle was the man who designed our generation'. This remark from Alexander Lieberman captions his 1948 Vogue photograph of Raymond Loewy and his elegant wife Viola on the beach at St. Tropez. They seem to have the place to themselves, and their elegant cabin cruiser with a prominent American flag floats on the water behind them. The scene suggests the Californian dream to come in the 1950s, with Loewy ahead of the game.

Raymond Loewy was a French-born designer who found his way into product design largely by accident in New York in the 1930s. Once in, there was no stopping him. Cars, boats, trains, cigarette packs, biscuit boxes, oil company logos, office equipment: he put his talents to work on all of them, both in the 1930s and through into the 1950s. The first designer to get his picture on the cover of *Time* magazine, with the tag 'Loewy streamlines the sales curve', Loewy epitomises the invention of product design as a separate discipline in the USA, one linked directly to the marketing and image needs of large corporations. As such he is seen in opposition both to the Modernists, who evolved form from function, and to the craft tradition. Loewy's approach, however he may justify it, was all about the exterior appearance of objects. He had started in the USA as an illustrator on fashion magazines, and this concern with the appearance of objects he designed remained primary.

However, it must be said that the visual vocabulary he created, such as for Penn Rail locomotives, or later for Studebaker cars conveyed very directly and at times elegantly the aspirations of the consumers of the time. (It has even been argued that if Harold Vance, the president of Stude-

baker, had had more enthusiasm for sports cars then the
Starliner could have replaced the Ford Mustang as the most
popular sports car on the market). The stories Loewy relates in this book follow his design practice: he is constructing the Loewy image. From the elegant woman who
kisses the schoolboy in the train, to the bet as a fee for
redesigning the Lucky Strike pack, Loewy promotes Loewy.
The names of associates and fellow designers almost never occur: the only theoretical position adopted is the MAYA
slogan ('most advanced yet acceptable' – a notion as simplistic as it is meaningless).

A misleading and bombastic book, then? In some ways,
yes. But it conveys accurately the vigour, easy optimism
and directness of professional American design in the 1930s
and at the beginning of the 1950s. Even the odd, square
format, the quirky line drawings and the asymmetric typography mark the book out. But accuracy was never
Loewy's own strength: he had the advantage to outlive
most of his contemporaries such as Bel Geddes, Teague
and Dreyfuss, and continued to promote his version of history until his death. (Interestingly, *Never Leave Well Enough
Alone* was never published in the UK, while the French
edition was last reprinted in 1992. A lot of the material
was reused in Loewy's later *Industrial Design*). A more
balanced view of Loewy can be found in the Berlin exhibition catalogue of 1991, which deflates many of the myths
he created (in particular it brings out the role of his associates, and exposes some of his deliberate tricks, such as
turning up at NASA wearing a spacesuit and driving a con-
vertible, claiming to have driven over 70 miles through the
desert!) But at the height of Loewy's powers, the myths
worked, and his own writing brings this across.

Lines of Least Resistance

DONALD J. BUSH
THE STREAMLINED DECADE
George Braziller Inc., New York, 1975

One of the icons of American design of the late 1930s is Raymond Loewy's pencil sharpener. It is a chrome teardrop on a spindle, with a modest opening for the pencil. There is no handle or switch for the operation of the machine. In fact, it is only a prototype: the design was never put into production, and a number of the design problems (for example where to put the motor, how to remove the shavings, and even how to fix the thing to the desk) were therefore never resolved. For all that, the design has come in for a fair degree of obloquy, with remarks about supersonic pencils. For an object that exists in an edition of one, it has its own hall of fame.

Donald Bush's study of the streamlining movement in the 1930s does not mention Loewy's flight of fancy. He concentrates – correctly enough – on American transport design. Correctly, because it was in the USA, and particularly in the early design studios of Bel Geddes and Loewy that streamlining became the form of the norm. Studies of air resistance predate the twentieth century: Macquorn Rankin in 1864 is credited with producing the first theoretical drawings of streamlined forms, based on his research into hull shapes for ships, Streamlining became of serious interest only when new forms of transport – the motor car and the airplane in particular – offered the opportunity to exploit in practice earlier theoretical research. The streamlined trains, planes and automobiles of the 1930s do not only give the decade its visual style, however, but also an intellectual and aspirational one. Bush identifies the search for new visual forms with the search – which we might now characterise as naive – for a more perfect way of living. The books written by designers in this period – Bel Geddes's *Horizons* especially – underline the utopian aims of the streamlining movement, and Donald Bush's book underscores the importance of futuristic thinking as well as futuristic styling in the work of his designers. This movement, and its thinking, achieved its apogee in the 1939 New York World's Fair, when Bel Geddes's Futurama was one of the most popular exhibits.

Trains had a particular fascination for designers: Loewy designed for the Pennsylvania Railroad, Otto Kuhler for the Milwaukee Road, Henry Dreyfuss for the New York Central. And they also designed the interiors: the *twentieth Century Limited*, commemorated in a film of the same title, offered travel in Hollywood luxury. Appearance, however, was all: the weight of the iron shrouds often negated the streamlining effect on the train's performance. Their approach was quite different from European train designers and engineers such as Gresley or Chapelon, who looked to performance not appearance.

Bush links both the evolution of theoretical streamlining ideas and the commercial exploitation of these ideas to meet the consumer demands of 1930s America, culminating in the celebrations of the 1939 New York World's Fair. His book is a primary text on understanding the forces underlying the design of that decade.

Born in the USA

ARTHUR J. PULOS
THE AMERICAN DESIGN EXPERIENCE
THE AMERICAN DESIGN ADVENTURE
MIT Press, Boston, 1972

This pair of books by the American academic Arthur J. Pulos offers a measured reading of the course of American design in the twentieth century. The strength of Pulos's approach is that it links progress in industry and technology, markets and consumers, with the development of design practices, design education, exhibitions and design associations. His history of design institutions, and of the ways in which the design profession developed in a legal and fiscal framework, is particularly useful. He also covers both graphic and product design, and contemporary architecture, particularly in housing. As a source of detailed reference the books are excellent, and Pulos balances the different elements of his discourse with a firm hand. His approach has a certainty to it, a degree of confidence and development that did indeed characterise American self-perceptions in the period up to 1975 that he is studying.

Pulos adopts as a general standpoint the good design principles set out in Philip Johnson and Charles Eames's famous series of exhibitions at the Museum of Modern Art in New York. These had as their aim to match good functional values with existing or prototype products across a wide range of fields. It is an open question what exact influence these designs had on consumers, but they were certainly not lost on the coming generation of design teachers and students. A number of early reputations – for example that of the Eames – were hastened along by these exhibitions. While Pulos supports the good design position,

Chrysler Airflow, 1934

he is not judgemental about it, giving space to the work of other designers in drawing a broad canvas.

But the postulate of inevitability hidden in the canon of good design – its rightness and so its inevitability – does have its effect on his text. He seems to miss the chaos, excitement and uncertainties which must have in fact held sway in manufacturing and design in the period, the moments of chance, luck and circumstance which make up the actual pattern of events, and do not make it run to a prescribed course. He is, of course, aware of the hype and even cynicism at work in design in certain sectors, such as the automobile industry (his handling of Harley Earl's work at General Motors is particularly good). But when it comes to post-modernism and anti-design his system fails him. This falls out of the main scope of his text.

Pulos's deterministic approach is reflected in the design and layout of the book. Rigorously modern sans-serif type, set ragged in narrow columns, on a vertically accentuated format. The illustrations, all in black and white, are well chosen and deftly used. The publishers, MIT Press, make an important contribution to the literature on design and architecture of the 1980s and 1990s, and these elegant and useful books are a fine example of their craft.

Classical positions

WALTER DORWIN TEAGUE
DESIGN THIS DAY
The Technique of Order in the Machine Age
The Studio, London, 1946

The rhetorical, almost biblical flavour of the title chosen by Teague is a good indication of the man. For him 'the new profession of industrial design' was one 'in which one man of restless mind and many interests assembles around him a group of variously trained co-workers'. Photographs show him at his desk facing rows of ordered drawing boards and white-shirted, short-haired designers, like a Victorian clerk supervising his counting house. He certainly played the patriarchal role: asked in the early 1950s by Boeing to consult on the interior design of the first transatlantic jets, he built a full scale model which he used to demonstrate the new fittings and cabin procedures. His description of the 707 as 'my aircraft' riled the Boeing engineers considerably. In 1941, he defended himself in a test income tax action by claiming design was exempt as a profession, not taxable as a vulgar trade. (When Raymond Loewy was told that Teague was going to be chosen for this test case, which affected the tax status of other designers, he was horrified: 'You've made Teague the *first* American industrial designer', he cried!)

In his book, published in the USA in 1940 and in a revised edition in the UK in 1947, he develops his idea of design as a noble calling, tracing its origins back to the Greek master builders of the Parthenon. He puts a deliberate distance between this scholarly approach and the flamboyant directness of his fellow designers such as Loewy or Bel Geddes. Teague never had the same public reputation as his fellows, but he did a considerable body of solid, well-respected work for major clients such as Kodak, Dupont and Ford. There is, though, a sense through this book of petulance, of the author not being accorded his place, even of not being in the correct place. Its argument for designers as an elite profession, keepers of the mysteries, has something of William Morris in it. The revisions and extensions made after the Second World War also read like shoring up the dike against populism. The long analysis of traditional Golden Section forms, which Teague sees as the mainspring of his classical approach to design, reads more as an academic text than as a rationale for a career. He does, however, cite modern examples such as the Hoover dam and monoplane aircraft construction among contemporary examples, and demonstrates the breadth of learning he cites for an ideal designer.

I once asked Dorwin Teague's son about his father's rather distant vision, as it seemed to me. He told me that his father had always seen designers as being parallel to architects, and was perhaps saddened that they did not have the same respect. In fact, he told me, his father had studied architecture and qualified as an architect late in his life, and it was one of the achievements of which Teague Senior was most proud. This preference for architecture may have had another consequence. In the early 1950s Teague visited Italy (where every designer has first qualified as an architect) and wrote a report on the state of product design in the country. This report was extremely influential in waking up American curators, editors and designers to the developments in Italy, where Teague must have enjoyed talking to 'fellow-architects'.

Structures on the Silver Screen

DONALD ALBRECHT

DESIGNING DREAMS
Thames & Hudson, London

'Our ideas of foreign places are formed long before we see them, from accounts and images that may well be fictional' Umberto Eco once said, 'and those images may be stronger and better than truth'. For many Europeans the image of America was that created by Hollywood, whether in the westerns of John Ford or the urban dramas of Wilder and Capra. For me, my first images came from the Fred Astaire and Gingers Rogers musicals that the BBC seemed to consider appropriate Sunday afternoon viewing in the late 1950s – my bit of escapism before the grim return to prep school. The modernistic sets with their angular steel and leather furniture, planar windows, open stairways and absence of decoration were pure modernism, to ten-year old eyes.

Donald Albrecht's project began with an exhibition comparing modern architectural and interior drawings and designs in the Museum of Modern Art, New York, with film stills from the same period. What emerged was an exhibition on how the cinema, especially Hollywood, used and even promoted modern architectural and interior design ideas. This book accompanied the exhibition. 'A major endeavour...'. he writes, 'is to explore the contrasts between the popular dreams realized in set designs... of the 1920s and 1930s... and the utopian visions expressed in the drawings and writings of modern architects'.

One of the reasons why Hollywood took up the modernist genre is that a lot of modernists ended up in Hollywood as a result of the migrations of the time: Joseph Urban, an architect of the Wiener Werkstatte, designed film sets for Hearst's Cosmopolitan Pictures, and Poiret's disciple Paul

Iribe for Cecil B. De Mille. Fritz Lang brought his own talents to Hollywood as did many others. One of the values of this book is in reminding us of the contribution of designers such as Vincent Korda, Cedric Gibbons, Alfred Junge and Paul Nelson.

Albrecht makes the point that in Hollywood's hands the utopian visions of the Bauhaus or the Werkstatte became distorted. Modern architecture and interiors had been used in 'art' films in France, notably by Mallet-Stevens for Marcel L'Herbier and Lazare Meerson for René Clair, and in Germany by Lang and Wiene. In California, they were used for popular pictures, and the utopian visions became night clubs, beach houses, tycoon's offices and luxury hotels. Modernism was meant to equal luxury, high living, even decadence and vice. (In Hawks's *Bringing Up Baby* there is a deliberate change of set style as Katharine Hepburn moves from the city (chic apartment and luxury restaurant) to the country (solid traditional farmhouse, even if with some modern touches) and so to mark her change of character from frivolous to serious).

There were technical reasons why modernist interiors worked well in film, especially monochrome film, which are not lost on Albrecht. They also had a suitable anonymity for an increasingly international market for film. But while this book is good on detail, it does not perhaps explore the surrounding social ethos and attitudes towards modern architecture sufficiently to explain why film-goers enjoyed and apparently expected an on-screen design they would probably oppose at home. Nor is their brief period of glory accounted for (for such films disappear after the mid-1930s, according to Albrecht), given the success of *The Fountainhead* in 1949, perhaps the classic American film about modern architecture.

Burning Chrome

STEPHEN BAYLEY
HARLEY EARL
Wiedenfeld & Nicolson, London, 1980

'Who do your think you are, Mister Earl' went the first
line of the song, 'and how was it that you pinched my girl'.
Whether the songwriter had ever heard of Harley Earl, Head
of Styling at General Motors in the 1950s and early 1960s
no-one knows, but his staff at GM – who called their big,
sharp-suited and bullying boss 'Misterearl' had probably
heard it. It was Harley Earl who gave America a car worth
being seen cruising in, the streetlamp light bouncing off the
chrome baroque details and the flaring paint, the naugahyde
seat covers reflected in the streamlined dials, the raked screen
looking out over the long hood, covering an inefficient over-
powered engine bolted onto a dull, oversprung chassis. But
on the outside it looked great – and so did America.

It is easy to dismiss Earl as a stylist, a redneck borrower
of inappropriate design ideas for unconsidered functions:
monster tailfins and wrapped windscreens, jawlike radiator
grilles and bulbous bumpers. But how was it that someone
who should have been crafting the Batmobile was in fact
dictating policy for one of the largest motor manufacturers
in the world? Bayley's account links the prosperity and vision of post-war America with the realities of insatiable consumer demand and the cynical exploitation of a market.
Earl's curious but personal vision was in tune with the right
sector of the market, however appalling it may seem to different sensibilities, however much it may divorce form and
any idea of function.

Earl held up a mirror to American middle-class society – it
was a chromed curved bumper, and so the reflection was,
in fact if not in appearance, flawed. With the collapse of

American self-confidence after Vietnam and Watergate, the projected image no longer held true, and car design, in time, changed to follow suit. So long as what was good for General Motors was good for America, Earl's vision held sway.

This book was first published in 1980 from Weidenfeld and Nicolson, in a large, illustrated format. I later reissued it in the Trefoil Design Heroes series, and Grafton published it in paperback in 1992. Its publishing history is an interesting paradigm of design publishing in the 1980s and 1990s. When the book first appeared, Harley Earl was an unknown, except among American car enthusiasts, and the grand format was necessary. A decade later, Earl's name had even featured in a UK beer commercial, and so a small format inexpensive reissue was possible, followed by a mainstream paperback edition. Much of this success was due to the coruscating quality of Bayley's writing, and the real enthusiasm that showed through his rollercoaster prose. Bayley (and others) brought the tenets of the New Journalism into writing on design, and helped in the process that through the 1980s turned design from a minor subject into a major one.

Cadillac Fleetwood Sedan, 1959

Ruined church near Verdun, 1917

Wars & Walls

Souvenir Swastikas

NAZI KITSCH
Exhibition catalogue, Darmstadt, 1975

This is a small illustrated book of Nazi memorabilia and
artefacts published in Darmstadt in 1975. The items illustrated – thimbles, cufflinks, ashtrays and matchboxes
decorated with swastikas, commemorative Fuhrertag mugs,
tin whistles in red and black – are portrayed without comment, presumably to emphasize the intellectual hollowness
of Nazi doctrines, and so should be taken, in line with the
theme of the exhibition, as proof that Nazi equals Kitsch,
that National Socialism could not inspire more than the ba-
nal in the decorative arts. And because we can laugh at its
pretensions, then we do not have to take it too seriously.
Some of the objects are absurd: hairgrips with marcasite
swastikas on the end, a red Christmas tree holder in the
swastika shape (for once a reasonably ergonomic use for the
hakenkreuz).

To put the theme of this booklet in context, we should remember that two years earlier the important *Kunst im
Dritten Reich* exhibition has been held in Cologne. The title came from the Nazi's own exhibition in Munich in 1937
that presented official Nazi art. In 1973 for the first time
since 1945 some of the masterpieces of Nazi art – the
heroic naturalism and idealised Aryan figures in the works
of Kampf, Ziegler, Breker and others – were brought up
from the cellars. These were displayed alongside enlarged
photographs of real life under the Nazis. This was an excellent and laudable first attempt to confront publicly the
visual nature of the Nazi regime – even if it was done rather too didactically for some critics, who felt the contrast
between the photos and the works of art was unnecessary,
and for others who felt that displaying anything that glori-
fied Nazism was an obscenity. With *Nazi Kitsch* this second critical hesitation is understandable. The publication

bears a curious – and perhaps deliberate – resemblance to a series of British books that began with *The English Sunrise* (Matthews Millar Dunbar, 1969). These used the same square landscape format, with unannotated images, to provide a lifestyle mirror to the eccentricities and absurdities of English taste. Later volumes dealt with subjects like Afghan trucks and Chinese paper cut-outs. Presenting these folksy or *art brut* curiosities as visual delectation was a publishing novelty, and they sold deservedly well. Using this means to present Nazi work is more suspect, though there is a foreword by Rolf Steinberg and a documentary appendix. In approaching the Nazi era, any fascination needs must be mixed with horror, and an awareness of the profound evil of the Hitler régime – and all its works – must underpin our laughter at its absurdities.

Two more recent publications put this awareness into context. The first is *Selling Hitler*, Robert Harris's joyous and irreverent account of the Hitler Diaries scandal, in which a gullible journalist and an artful, somewhat larger-than-life forger took a major German publishing house, and numerous Western newspapers and magazines (including the London *Sunday Times* and the historian Lord Dacre) for an expensive and ridiculising ride over spurious diaries kept by Hitler, and miraculously saved after the war. But behind the enjoyable spectacle of the men in suits being caught out by their own greed, there looms the darker picture of a vigorous market in Nazi memorabilia, and an enthusiasm for the artefacts (dubious or not) of the Third Reich. And if we want to understand the background of *Nazi Kitsch*, a good starting point is Daniel Jonah Goldhagen's *Hitler's Willing Executioners* (Alfred Knopf, 1996). The book uses contemporary and postwar documents to show how it was not the dedicated members of the SS alone who were responsible for mass killings, but how the programme of the Final Solution was tacitly (or even actively) endorsed by everyday Germans, who were not Nazi party members. For all the disputes over the book, it is a salutary warning about the relationship between political and moral authority, through its depiction of a nation that accepts dictatorship and its consequences.

Hush, here comes a whizz-bang

GERALD PAWLE

THE SECRET WAR

Harrap & Co., London, 1956

The damage war has done to humanity, society and culture in the twentieth century is endless and incalculable. Hobsbawm in *Age of Extremes* uses the term 'Age of Catastrophe' for the period 1914 to 1945. He draws particular attention to the fact that global war involved all the social and economic resources of the participants. This inevitably includes design and technology. In Germany, lack of specific resources (coffee and petrol are two examples) led to a programme of improvisation and innovation in finding new fuels and foods, and at the same time a whole range of new weapons (including the first jet fighter aircraft, manned rockets and guided missiles) were developed and introduced. In the USA new systems for ship and aircraft building created new towns around factories and changed the demographic basis of America in the process. In the UK technical developments, such as the (pre-war) invention of radar, were to change many aspects of warfare, while on the 'home front' concepts such as 'utility furniture' introduced new ideas of design to a wider, if not so willing, market.

This book deals with one section of the design and engineering developments in warfare in Britain during the Second World War. It is an informal history of the Admiralty's Department of Miscellaneous Weapons Development, the 'Wheezers and Dodgers' as they called themselves. Created in the aftermath of the disaster at Dunkirk (a retreat always seen by the British as a victory) and the appalling losses of merchant shipping to air and submarine attack, the DMWD pioneered everything that might help, from the sublime to the ridiculous, from a steam-powered anti-tank gun (hopeless) to a forward-throwing depth-charge launcher (excellent), from an invisible boat to a self-propelled Catherine Wheel loaded with half a ton of amatol explosive to breach sea defences. The projects are always makeshift, as if accepting the realities of a total war were unacceptable.

Pawle's account of the DMWD's activities is straight boffin-land (they were mad about rockets, for example, often with hilarious consequences). The scientists were always absent-minded, falling off piers and tapping live shells with hammers: their ideas involved simple things like building airbases on icebergs. One project involved throwing a Jeep out of an aircraft, and relying on the braking effect of rockets to ensure a safe landing: only several Jeeps later are the inherent instabilities of the project realised. To give them credit, much of the work was done in desperation, and many of the stories are truly funny, in retrospect. The book makes a virtue of the British notion of improvisation, and so demeans the role of real research, science and design in solving problems. The tone of the book is always 'what jolly fun, with the Hun at the gates'. But read in parallel with something like Thomas Pynchon's stark, not to say Byzantine, novel *V*, or Cronin's sober and realistic *The Small Back Room*, *The Secret War* becomes a testament to English amateurism − and lack of vision.

Pawle's book is, at one level, a sobering account of the contempt for serious research and innovation that was to plague post-war industry in the UK for decades. None of the technologies that the war helped to develop and which had a long-term future, such as jet propulsion, radar and computing, ever came within the orbit of the Wheezers and Dodgers, and it is difficult to see what such a band would have made of them. For a clearer picture of serious science at war, there are R.V. Jones's memoirs *A Scientist's War,* which, it must be said, also contains a fair number of jokes.

Ready-mythed Concrete

PAUL VIRILIO
BUNKER ARCHAEOLOGY
Princeton Architectural Press, New York, 1994

In 1940 a camouflage officer was being shown round part
of Southern Command in England by a colleague, who in
civilian life had been a famous theatrical set designer. His
pride and joy was a defensive pillbox disguised as a thatched
cottage. 'Very good!', the visiting officer wrote in his diary
that evening, 'if the Germans ever invade, they'll never know
it's a pillbox – but if they know anything about the English
theatre they'll know it's designed by him!'. In the 1940s in
Britain the conventional form of fixed defence was via the
sham – trucks despised tanks, guns made out drain pipes.
At first this was for lack of the real thing, later it became
away of misleading or confusing the enemy, an approach
that echoes Cornford's famous definition of propaganda.

On the other side of the Channel the Germans were creating a real defence, real guns and real concrete and real steel.
Today there are perhaps two architectural and design camps
in Britain and Europe: those whose perspective stretches only
into a narrowly defined past, borrowing old motifs to sham
new contexts, and those for whom real technology is a way
of solving real problems. So the publication of *Bunker Ar-
chaeology* comes in English at an apt time, even if it is 20
years since the book's first publication in French.

This book analyses German defences of the Atlantic Wall,
the watchtowers, artillery positions, U-boat pens and case-
mates, constructed from the northern frontiers of Holland
down to the Spanish border. Much of the work was done
by forced labour, and the architect of the overall plan was
Albert Speer, who took over day to day running of the pro-

gramme after Fritz Todt's mysterious death in a plane crash in 1942.

Virilio's very personal text explores the contradictions inherent in this monstrous architecture, through its rare monolithic quality, its invasion of conventions of defence, and its overthrow not so much by force of arms but by new definitions of military space. The architectural qualities of the constructions are conveyed through the author's own dramatic photographs. Their continuing relation to our own definitions of power and enclosure is subtly argued. Virilio is an urban planner and cultural theorist; only superficially is this a book about strategic warfare. His central point is that the Atlantic Wall represented not only the frontier of Nazi expansion but also the limits of their thinking. Intellectually, as well as militarily, the bunker was a final point of conflict, a schwerpunkt. It is this perception of how architecture operates under extreme circumstances that gives his text its contemporary relevance. Thus the text and images offer a commentary on the modern state and the modern city that is even more relevant now than it was when first published, and remains wholly free of nostalgia for the concrete relics, and wholly free of sham.

This edition contains a new commentary on developments between 1945 and 1990, pointing out how the creation of a different military spatial order by the first V2 rockets has accelerated into new concepts of military territory through the strategic defence initiative and the end of the Cold War. Thus his book asks us to look at the limits of design and architectural thinking, and derive our understandings from parallel historical and social processes. The Atlantic Wall failed because it defined conflict in the wrong terms: while this is not to deny the bravery of those who fought it, it is a salutary reminder of the limits of thinking.

Modesty under Tension

PETER RICE
AN ENGINEER IMAGINES
Artemis, London, 1996

Some years ago I proposed to a firm of architectural publishers a book with the intended title *Engineering takes command*. The editor approached was appalled by title, but not,
it turned out, because of the rather obvious pun on Giedion's
famous book, but because of the possible 'offence' implied
in it. I hope neither architects nor engineers nor designers
will be put off, and certainly not offended by the title of
Peter Rice's posthumous autobiography, *An engineer imag-
ines*. As an account of the work of one of the most important figures in late twentieth century architecture alone it
deserves attention, as well as for what Peter Rice has to
say about the role of the engineer in contemporary practice.

The book opens with an account of the design and building of the Centre Beaubourg, the project which first brought
Peter Rice to the notice of a wider public, though he had
earlier done important work on the Sydney Opera House.
Later chapters describe this project, as well as the Menil
Gallery in Houston, the Lloyd's building in London, and
the Théâtre de la Pleine Lune in France. Other chapters are
more reflective, looking at the problems of working with
industry, the challenge of working with different architects
simultaneously on differing projects, on his work with Ren-
zo Piano for Fiat, and on such subjects as architecture and
photography, his respect for mentors such as Ove Arup and
Jean Prouvé, and the pleasures of horseracing. The important essay on the role of the engineer has been previously
published elsewhere, but is here revised and extended. The
effect of the whole book is of modesty shot through with

genius, combined with a clear understanding of the real role the modern engineer can play in architecture, and of limitations. What also shines through the what is Rice's own quixotic, very Irish personal character and charm.

For 'engineers need identity', Peter Rice tells us. 'Engineers need to be known as individuals responsible for the artefacts they have designed'. His own astonishing, though tragically short career as an engineer working with architects has helped to start making this happen, and this book will do much to further the cause. But Rice is not making a case for the public adulation of engineers in the Brunel or Eiffel tradition. Rather he is talking about engineers' understanding of their own worth, and their being willing to stand up and take credit for it.

This is an elegant and important book; it deserves to be widely read for what has to say about the past, and for what it has to say about the future.

(Since writing this review [first published in *World Architecture* in 1996], it turns out that the Centre Beaubourg is to host a major exhibition on The art of the engineer, from Eiffel to Rice. While the man himself might or might not appreciate this late accolade, it is certainly the case that his support for the importance of the contemporary engineer will find proper endorsement in the exhibition. It is perhaps a pity that in the design community there has not always been such a proper understanding of the solid values of modesty.)

Stressful Times

HENRI LEMOINE, PIERRE XERCAVINS,
BERNARD MARREY (EDITORS)
EUGENE FREYSSINET, UN AMOUR SANS LIMITE
Editions du Linteau, Cherbourg, 1993

The image of the engineer as a heavy man, plain-speaking, direct, uncouth even and certainly Scots, is enshrined in Kipling and paid homage to in *Star Trek*, and reflected in the adage that if the English ruled the British empire the Scots had built it for them. Why we expect engineers to look like their trade (in the way cooks from Chaucer to Jeanette Winterson have to be fat) is unknown, but probably related to a sense of nominative determinism that makes us satisfied that the world's first working aeroplane was built by the Wright brothers, or that Joseph Babey is a paediatrician and David Bird an ornithologist). The determinative that could be applied to Eugene Freyssinet is 'frisson', that physical sense of risk, and perhaps it would be appropriate.

Aircraft hangar, Orly, 1923

Freyssinet was born in Corréze in 1879 He studied at the Ecole Polytechnique in Paris and the Ecole Nationale des Ponts et Chaussées in Paris before he was apprenticed to the engineer Rabut. He served as an engineer in the French Army from 1904 to 1907 and was conscripted in 1914 until the 1918 Armistice. Between these two periods in the army he worked as a road engineer for local authorities in Central France, building bridges and viaducts. From 1918 until 1928 he worked as Technical Director for the Société des Enterprises Limousin in Paris, being responsible in particular for the concrete aircraft hangars at Orly (1923, destroyed by bombing 1944), and in 1929 he established his own practice.

But this simple narrative conceals a guiding obsession: he had become convinced in 1913 of the potential of pre-stressed concrete as a building material, especially for civil engineering works. While reinforced concrete (as used at Orly) was an established material, early attempts at pre-stressing concrete had failed, and Freyssinet's ideas were ridiculed. When he returned to working on the idea in 1924, everyone, starting with his employer and close friend Claude Limousin, told him he was trying to solve an insoluble problem, and wasting his time and money by going it alone, at the age of fifty, to try a material everyone said would fail.

Limousin was almost right: Freyssinet's first (and for a while only) customer was an electricity supply company who wanted concrete pylons. As Freyssinet says in one of the pieces reproduced in this book, 'about the only thing you cannot make economically from pre-stressed concrete is a pylon'. While technically a brilliant success, the pylons almost bankrupted him, and his proposal for bridges were often turned down flat by sceptical planners. However, in 1934 he won the chance to arrest the subsidence of the Gare Maritime in the harbour at Le Havre in northern France. This enormous warehouse was built in reinforced concrete with one wall founded on rock, the other three on mud and clay, which were in turn affected by the rise and fall of the Channel tides. Despite preliminary tests that showed the proposed construction would be stable, once built the outer wall and floor started dropping at a rate of nearly a centimetre a month. With one wall fixed, collapse was imminent. No-one else had a solution to propose, so, as Freyssinet says 'it was worth risking everything'. His solution, based on reinforcing pillars in pre-stressed concrete, worked, and Freyssinet's reputation began to rise. With the construction of enormous caissons for the docks at Brest a few years later, the role and potential of pre-stressed concrete was established. Freyssinet's patents, previously rejected as unfeasible, were granted. The first licence he sold to make prestressed concrete earned him a million francs. This book brings together a number of texts and speeches by Freyssinet (who had always intended to write a biography, and even sketched out a plan which ran to nine volumes), together with an appreciation by Henri Lemoine, the former technical director of STUP, Freyssinet's company. From the latter we learn that Freyssinet did not hesitate to call a fool a fool if he thought it the right term, but that he was dedicated, hard-working and fair. From his own speeches it becomes clear that he did not mind reminding everyone that he had been right and the others wrong, though he is generous in his praise of his collaborators.

Freyssinet's career, with its frissons of risk, echoes in its dedication that of another French engineer, André Chapelon, the steam locomotive designer. He subjected the traditional 'rule of thumb' design of steam engines to a rigorous scientific analysis, which enabled him to design locomotives with higher performance and lower coal consumption. Just as the Wright brothers had realised that power not weight was the key to a feasible aircraft, Chapelon understood that maximising the energy of steam (by maintaining temperature and pressure) was the key to locomotive design. He even designed in the 1950s a locomotive capable of pulling a passenger train at 125 mph.

But the French railways (Société Nationale des Calamités Francais, as Chapelon later termed them) had decided, in step with the government's nuclear energy policy, to move to an electrified main line system. Chapelon's riposte was to demonstrate that one of his P 241 series locomotives could run from Paris to Lyon with the same load as an electric one, in less time and using less energy. He was summarily dismissed from his post as head of research and the locomotives he was working on were broken up for scrap. He got a quiet revenge: when the French started designing high speed trains some years later, they had problems with track handling and stability, and so asked Chapelon for help. He dug out the data he had created in the 1920s and solved their problems: and never once said 'I told you so!'

The status of engineers in French society is rather different from that of the oil-stained Scots of English literature. Chapelon looked like a prosperous banker, Freyssinet like a university professor. This respect for science can be seen in the continuing prominence of the long-established Grands Ecoles and from the de Gaulle period, with ints emphasis on technocracy. And it's worth remembering that Britain most famous father and son engineers, the Brunels, were also French in origin.

Sony MiniDisc system, 1996

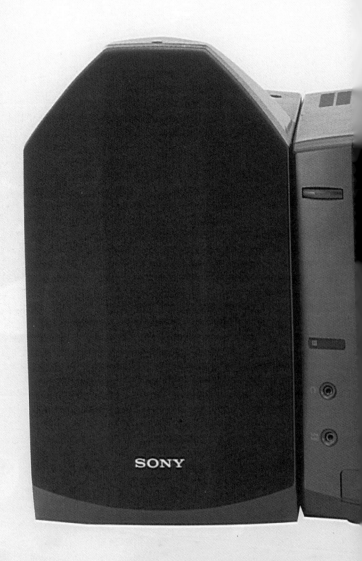

Oriental Perspectives

Dreams of the Past

Junichiro Tanizaki
In'ei Raisan (A Homage to Shadows)
Keizai Ourai, Tokyo, 1933

'What I am trying to show is that the shape itself of an apparently insignificant object can have an infinity of repercussions'. Tanizaki cites the fountain pen: suppose it had been invented in Japan, he argues, then it would not have had a steel nib but a brush. This would have written in Chinese ink on Japanese paper, and the arrival of the Western fountain pen would have had no impact on Japanese culture. But Western pens, by offering more in the form of a continuous ink supply, have created pressures, out of all proportion to their quality, for the abandonment of Japanese written characters and traditional materials, and so for the larger adoption of Western ideas by default.

This is particularly true, he continues, in the case of the traditional Japanese interior, where shade and darkness play a more important role than light, natural or artificial. For Tanizaki, the centre of the Japanese house is the *toko no ma*, the traditional alcove, once a bedroom, but now used to display a work of art or a seasonal floral decoration. Such treasures should be glimpsed as much as seen, like the fleeting and sombre decoration of a lacquer dish seen through the swirl of *miso* soup. And the work displayed is judged not on its own, but on its contribution to the whole ensemble, to the nuances of colour and shade of the *toko no ma* itself, its contents and its surroundings. This argument, of the essential and subtle values of light and shade in Japanese culture as opposed to Western, ranges across architecture, cuisine, theatre and artefacts. One main theme of the book is the beauty of Japanese women, their darkened teeth and whitened faces ideal to be seen in the obscurity of the *toko no ma*.

But Tanizaki, best known as a novelist and literateur, whose published work spans fifty years from 1910 onwards, was not the conservative this brief description of his ideas might suggest. Indeed his early fiction was regularly attacked for its modernism, especially in the portrayal of women, and as a translator of Oscar Wilde Tanizaki was once again attacked as pro-Western. One of his best-known novels, *A Mad Love*, deals with a relationship between a Japanese couple in the 1930s who are determined to be as 'Western' as possible, learning for example to dance the foxtrot and the charleston, but when their relationship fails unable to use either Western or traditional Japanese values to resolve their problems. So Tanizaki sees Western influence as a fact which in turn impinges on the values of Japanese society. His attitude is pluralistic rather than nostalgic, neither ultra liberal nor too conservative. Here he argues for retaining the best of Japanese tradition while accepting innovation, and not simply accepting tradition for tradition's sake (or new for newness' sake either). 'My aim in writing is to see if we can find some way of stopping the loss, and to revive this universe of shadows which we at risk of losing'.

Tanizaki's book is an interesting example of the vagaries of publishing: while an English edition appeared in the 1960s it was never widely distributed in the UK, and in the USA seems to have been read mainly by those interested in literature; his fiction still has an important place in twentieth century Japanese literature. But mention *In Praise of Shadows* to a French architect or designer (the French edition is still in print) and the response is enthusiastic. Jean Nouvel told me that he learned much about ways in which to use light and shade from Tanizaki, and that the book deepened his understanding of Japanese architecture, design and culture. 'And', he added, 'the section on Japanese *chiottes* in the countryside is just wonderful'.

Rewards of the New

MORITAKA MATSUMARA, EDITOR IN CHIEF
BEST OF JAPAN
Innovations: Present and Future
Nikkei, Tokyo, 1987

These are Annual Awards for Creative Excellence, and include the range of electronic items – photocopiers and faxes,
computer hardware and software – and industrial products
from robots to digital watches – familiar to other awards.
But the thinking here is total – Nomura Securities Treas-
ury-Indexed Variable-Redemption Notes also received a High
Award for Excellence, along with self heating Sake cans by
Toyo Jozo, a new artificial fur "Furtastic', a disposable electric shaver by Minimum and a toy paw for cats from Bandai
(the toy ears and tail were not so successful in the marketplace). The energy and diversity of Japanese design and innovation is evident: the robotics selection alone includes several industrial models, a household toy, and a restaurant
robot, which will perform all the functions of a busy wait-
er 'while allowing for easy repairs and maintenance'. The
absence of traditional categories allows for anything – from
a new laminate for wrapping fish to an engine for the
H-1 space rocket – to be considered. This is the same attitude that brings all services – design, marketing and production – together so often at the beginning of a product
development, and allows unconventional ideas the chance to
see the light: the Sony Walkman is the case-study many cite
(it came into being before the period of these awards), but
the Toy Cat's Paw (980,000 sold in the first six months)
also came out of a chance idea from a worker in the development section of the company.

The role of Japan in postwar industry and design is seen
in crude terms as a period of tinny imitation followed by

clever imitation followed by smart marketing. What this scenario ignores are two aspects of the Japanese social tradition that have had a profound effect on the way Japanese business has operated and the initiatives it has taken. The first is the tradition of a family business that passes from generation to generation, and translates in the present in a willingness to take a long-term view in the development of a product or a market, as opposed to the short term view often preferred by Western companies or imposed on them by short-term banking systems. This shows through in the relative rates of investment in research and development between Japanese and Western companies, at least until the end of the 1980s. It also has other manifestations: a Japanese businessman who paid a record price for a Van Gogh painting did so to show a Japanese bank also interested in it that they should not have bankrupted his father fifty years before.

The second aspect, which is less well documented, is that in traditional Japanese society artists whose work we now admire such as Hokusai and Hiroshige were seen as lowly artisans. The notions of copyright or artistic independence were nonexistent. The continuance of this, I feel, was an open attitude to the generation of ideas, and a lack of compartmentalisation between marketing, design, engineering and so on.

This open approach is reflected in the work selected for this book. Performance rather than image is the key factor, and the absence of preconceptions about 'good design' or 'right thinking' gives the selection both a certain vigour and a slightly surreal edge, by supplying a sideways slice of Japanese activities through Japanese eyes.

Asking Why Not

PAUL KUNKEL
DIGITAL DREAMS
The Work of the Sony Design Center
Universe, New York, 1999

A decade or so ago I was involved in editing a book on design management at the Dutch electronics company Philips, written by John Heskett. For the final chapter, which looked at the future for design within the company, we wanted to illustrate some future products. That proved a problem: there were plenty of exciting concept ideas around in the design offices, but not for public consumption – yet. So we ended up showing concepts that had been developed and then, for different reasons, not put into production. This was in fact the only time that Philips interfered with the content of the book, but it was still criticised on publication for its lack of independence.

The problem of authorial distance in writing about living subjects, whether individuals or corporations, is well known. In design books (and architectural ones) it is often today compounded by the fact that the subject controls rights to the images necessary to accompany any text. And among secretive design units, the Sony Research Center has a serious reputation: while other Japanese companies might submit concepts to magazines and annuals, Sony remained mute. Parts of the outline of the story of Sony could be gathered from the late Akio Morita's 1986 book *Made in Japan*, other ideas gathered from press releases and the products themselves. Morita, and his founding partner Masaru Ibuka realised from the start that new products would need new markets (and would in turn create further markets), and that delivery quality and satisfaction would have to be the basis for any long-term success. This is easy to say, and much harder to do, of course. What Sony achieved was to link consistent innovation in technology (particularly in miniaturisation) with the creation of consumer loyalty in expanding and competitive marketplaces. Sony fostered this approach through insisting on, and rewarding, quality in design.

An example of this is the project they called Sony Spirit. In the period 1988-89, when recession was the word in vogue – and in effect – and companies were retrenching on innovation, the Sony Design Center also stopped working on new projects. But they did so in order to spend several months creating 'blue-sky' projects that would redefine the spirit of Sony. The work that emerged (and is published here) such as Professional, Elegance, Tea Ceremony and Enigma, are not just exquisite formal statements. They also represent, visually, new analyses of how such products might be used, extended and developed in the future. None of them went into production, but that was not the object of the exercise. It was to get the imagination of the design Center refocussed for the upturn that was around the corner.

For what Sony have been particularly able to do is to manage innovation (the history of design and technology is full of people who could innovate but could not manage, and vice-versa). This process Kunkel calls 'what time is it?' Imagine the life-cycle of a new product line from its first introduction to its replacement in the market by a completely new product as a day. Sunrise is the first version, often 'built any way you can'. This first product begins to gain a market and redefine itself in the process, until around noon the 'iconic' version is achieved: the model that sums up its essential original goals in an effective size, performance, relationship to the media and user. From this point the product can be redefined for segment markets (sports models, children's models, lifestyle models, or whatever). If the product is strong enough, this afternoon of diversity will stretch into a perpetual sunset, where a product can be continuously redefined for new or expanding markets. But, almost inevitably, a new technology will emerge, and the product will reach market exhaustion. A classic example of this is the Sony Walkman's twenty-year run from its introduction in 1978. It achieved a classic form with the 1983 WM-20, then split across six or seven market ranges, distinguished by texture, functionality, styling, colour and even gender. And while still a major product, it is set to disappear behind the new MiniDisc technology. Kunkel runs this example across several of Sony's major product lines, and it is a very valuable analysis.

What Sony also realised was that technology that did not communicate its function or potential to the user was wasted technology. And if it did not speak the visual language the user wanted to see, it was also wasted effort. Thus Sony's insistence on product semantics goes beyond simple functionality into creating a valid personality for each product, and elements such as packaging design, control units and even logo design are designed to communicate the right values. Because, Sony realised, values migrate: a 'sports look' for a Walkman can be applied, not as a design solution but as a metaphor, to a portable telephone or miniature voice recorder. It is a process he calls 'turning product into myth'. The simplest expression of this is perhaps in the 'My First Sony' range for children, but it operates at more complex levels as well, between the Viao range of portable computers and Playstation games consoles for example, and into the new range of products that the digital age is empowering.

Kunkel tells these stories in great detail, with frequent quotes and comments from the designers involved. To achieve this he gained unparalleled access to the Design Center: they must have had confidence in him. And so he also in them. To write with understanding about such a creative and complex organisation, it is necessary to share its values with openness and enthusiasm, though not uncritically. And the quality of the insights he achieves validate this approach, even if it leaves some aspects untouched. There is even an answer to the question the cynic might raise 'why are Sony willing to tell the story now?' The answer is summed up by Nobuyuki Idei, the current CEO and head of Sony Design Center: 'the digital revolution will shake our entire business platform so that brand image, production power and even the best technology will no longer be enough. We must recognise that in the future most of our products will become part of a larger digital network. From now on, Sony's work is to build bridges between computers, communications and entertainment... not mere boxes'.

In other words, products will no longer be limited to specific functions, but be multi-functional and customisable. It is not merely a matter of combining a radio, stopwatch and mobile telephone in a sports grip for a jogger, but rather turning the product/function equation around, to think solutions first. This way, content not form becomes the key question, though its answer has to have affective qualities that reach out to the user. This requires not only new design strategies, but new corporate thinking on a global level. The former divisions and hierarchies of corporate structure will not fit the new pattern. But it is a fair bet that the Design Center – the dreamers at the heart of Sony – will still be in there, looking forward to a new world.

Alan Shephard returns from his historic suborbital space flight

Heroic America

Dominating Figures

MARTIN PAWLEY
BUCKMINSTER FULLER DESIGN HERO
Trefoil, London, 1990

To visit the Buckminster Fuller archive in California the
researcher needs pencil, paper – and a fork-lift truck. Fuller kept everything, and the documents for his life are stored,
in crates on pallets industrially – and industriously – racked
in a warehouse in Los Angeles. This omnivorous approach
is a true echo of Fuller's life: his own accounts of it read
like a catalogue of statistics – how many miles he has travelled, how often he has lectured, how many interviews he
has given His speeches and texts are crammed with information and extrapolation, prediction and prophecies of hope
and gloom. If there is a certain petulance in this, it is born
of the remarkable series of failures that make Buckminster
Fuller one of the most important design thinkers of the
middle twentieth century. Whether it was pressed wood
bricks, a three-wheeled car, or a portable house, all his
major practical projects turned to dust in his hands. Even
the geodesic dome at the Montreal Expo caught fire.

Richard Buckminster Fuller was born in 1895 into a prosperous and intellectual Massachusetts family. He died in
1982. The key period in his life was the year 1927-1928,
a year spent in silence after his dismissal from the Stock-
dale Brick Company, in which he developed his own very
personal vision of engineering and technology, based on
extensive and eclectic reading, and his own experiences in
industry and in the American Navy. Fuller's thinking as
an engineer and architect always looked beyond the conventional solution. The 4-D mast-supported house was ignored the established rules of building construction, just
as the Dymaxion car, launched in 1933 at the Chicago
World Fair, took automobile technology several decades

ahead of current practice. As a result of this forward vision (and his lack of formal credentials) his ideas were treated with ridicule: the AIA turned down ungraciously his offer of a free patent on the 4-D design, and the Dymaxion car company failed after press outcry following a fatal accident. The same result befell his Wichita house, developed from a portable cabin used by the US Army, and seen as a great hope for rehousing post-war America.

Pawley's approach is to disentangle the different strands that make up the Fuller story, particularly over the original titling and sequence for the early 4-D and Dymaxion proposals. This on its own is a major contribution, but the main strength of the book is the author's evident empathy with his subject. Martin's own definition of a hero involves failure as well as success (one of his personal heroes is the yacht designer Arthur Piver, who disappeared at sea on one of his own trimarans), and Fuller's endless struggles against disaster (some of his own making, notably the Wichita house) meet this requirement excellently.

And ironically, without the disasters, there would have been no Buckminster Fuller. Had he achieved a reputation only as a car or house designer, he would have been just a footnote. His need to express himself against disaster, his broad approach to technology and society, his total vision of an ephemeralised society achieved through information, are what makes him a figure of the first rank. Had he lived to the age of a hundred, he would have seen much of what he had prophesied coming about: though not exactly, how or why, he had predicted it. He was, though, remembered in the word buckminsterfullerene, an iscoshedronic molecule of carbon, structured like a geodesic dome, discovered in 1985: it is one of the most stable forms of carbon, probably the most proliferating and possibly the oldest. The discovery has led to the unearthing of similar structures, known colloquially to scientists as buckyballs. Perhaps he'd have liked that too.

Classing the Masters

JAY DOBLIN
ONE HUNDRED GREAT PRODUCT DESIGNS
Van Nostrand Reinhold, New York 1970

Jay Doblin worked as a designer for Raymond Loewy, before going to Chicago where he became the head of design at IIT and later of his own design consultancy. This book is the result of a twenty year programme with his students, to establish through peer group selection the hall of fame of American design. Working designers and design teachers were regularly asked to name 'classic' products, and the results of these polls were sifted down into this book.

The intentions were excellent, the method interesting, but the results are flat. All the products selected – the Eames

Eames Lounge Chair, 1956

furniture (the largest representation by a single designer), the Franklin stove and the Winchester rifle (in a bow to vernacular origins), the Olivetti typewriters and IBM computers (from the land of the skyscraper office) – are seriously worthy of inclusion. Few could argue that they do not represent good design, however that is defined (though Doblin's definition is a narrow one). But there is none of the challenge or surprise that a more eclectic and individual selection would have stimulated. The interest of the book lies rather in the informed comments that Doblin himself makes on the background to products and their designers, and in the real sense his text generates of a family of mainly American designers at work to a common end. And in this the book reflects the involved and caring face that the 1960s and 1970s generation of designers, in America as in Europe, were so anxious to present, after the hard sell of the 1950s and before.

The notion of a Hall of Fame is borrowed from American sports such as baseball.Baseball, with its extreme level of rules and structures, and its fascination with production and output figures, mirrors in some ways the industrial system that developed in the American north-east, where the game began: it is an essentially urban game, as is basketball. In the same way the Hall of Fame is an attempt to create an immediate history for a new sport: the idea of maximum effort leading to fame has another industrial version, in the Stakhanovite heroes of Soviet industry, another attempt at instant history. Doblin's use of the idea can therefore be read in two ways: an attempt to create a history of American design (in a country aware of the absence of collective histor) and as an attempt to validate the achievements of American design througfh an impartial analysis, similar to thesurveys of market research which underpinned so much of the commercial development of the USA during the 1950s and 1960s. The idea of an objective historical canon of design, validated by research, may today seem inappropriate, but for a profession seeking to justify its place it had a certain attraction.

Fragments of Fame

ANDY WARHOL
ANDY WARHOL'S INDEX (BOOK)
Random House, New York, no date.

The fluorescent colours, the oversized dot, the simplified but familiar image of the soup tin or the starlet. Often imitated, never bettered, as the advertising slogan goes, Warhol's graphic design was the first vehicle for his international stardom: in parallel with is interminable films (often made in his name by Paul Morissey) and happenings and events at his Manhattan Factory. This is the 1960s Warhol, before the later white shock of hair in the wheelchair, only relict of the one-person Society for Cutting Up Men. And at the end of the 1980s, the Diaries, everyone's chance to find out if they had been 'famous for fifteen minutes' in Warhol's terms. A definition of fame that involved only presence, not achievement, being here, not doing anything. Such a definition can, with sufficient pretension (Andy? Pretentious?), be linked back to the Sartrean distinction between *être* and *nèant*.

Andy Warhol's *Index* is therefore something of a throwback, seen today. For example, it has content (in the Jean-Luc Godardian sense – a beginning, a middle and an end, but not necessarily in that order), unlike much of his later work. (Whatever his film of the Empire State Building during 24 hours had, content it did not.) There are photographs and texts (not necessarily related to each other), a few popups, a floppy 45 rpm record, and even a free balloon. There is an overall monochrome, soft-edged printing, colour only as fluorescents. No jacket, only a cover in thick plastic with a woolly image cached within (Brillo pads and Chairman Mao in soft-focus 3-D.) The images are mainly grainy monochromes of the denizens of

The Factory, as he called his studio. The text is mainly a persistent interview with a German reporter who only gets monosyllables out of Warhol, and ambiguous ones at that. But there is humour, of a kind: a two-page popup of a mock-mediaeval castle, with jousting knights (and the Three Musketeers stagecoach) in the foreground, like something from a children's book, is labelled 'We'er constantly attacked' (it is the only image in the book with a caption). So for all the heavy black images, the *Index,* in documenting at random the activities of his tribe, has a certain enthusiasm and energy, which contradicts the bleak ambiguities of his later pieces.

So is this Warhol before his descent into visible absence, or Warhol prefiguring his later discovery of the positivism of anonymity? This is the question still debated about Andy, best summarised as 'did he know what he was doing' or did he just do it? Was he a recorder of the anomie of urban America – or at least its New York underbelly – or a prophet? In one sense, pace the commentators, the question is irrelevant. Warhol's deliberately empty work, devoid of *auteur*, actors (apart from his superstars) and often action, acts as a mirror, in which we can see whatever forms we prefer. His skill was to create a total mirror, an ur-glass in which both our fears and fantasies had equal place, in which we could find both nadir and nirvana. And maintain the self-created, self-perpetuated Warhol legend, which, I suspect, was his ultimate intention. And the *Index* has no index, of course, just a couple of pages of white paper at the end, with 'blank' written on them in black crayon.

California Dreaming

JOHN NEUHART, MARILYN NEUHART, RAY EAMES
EAMES DESIGN
The Work of the Office of Charles and Ray Eames
Harry N. Abrams, Inc., New York, 1989

Charles and Ray Eames, the American designers who created the 1950s California Style of design, saw themselves as
designers with a mission. Charles had studied with Eero
Saarinen, a Modernist Finnish emigre, even if one whose
personal vision was never fully integrated into the Miesian
formalities of later architectural pretensions, and Ray under Hans Hofmann, a German artist adept at abstraction.
They met at the Cranbrook Academy, where Saarinen taught,
and married in 1940. Charles had had some architectural
work before the war, and during the war had worked on
developing splints and stretchers from moulded plywood
for the US Navy. Their major opportunity in architecture
came with the invitation to build a case study house for
the Californian architectural magazine *Arts & Architecture*,
for which they had already designed covers and special projects.

Having decided to create a home from standard industrial parts, they promptly redesigned the building once the
elements were delivered, creating in the process what was
to become an icon of the modern American home. At the
same time, Charles' experiments with moulded plywood
furniture, exhibited at the Museum of Modern Art in New
York, had attracted the eye of Herman Miller, for whom
he went on to design a stunning series of works. Both
Charles and Ray collaborated on these projects and a range
of exhibitions and films, on themes as diverse as the circus, the Algerian insurrection, jellyfish and the power of
mathematics.

The Eameses are still design icons for many in the American design community. I myself have met one hard-boiled American design manager, otherwise emotionally pithed out, who cried at the sight of Ray accepting an award in her late husband's name. Now it is true that many of Charles's designs are rightly among the design icons of the century, and that their exhibition work encapsulated an ideal view of suprematist America in the 1950s and 1960s. That America needs heroes is well known – Hollywood has taught us that – but why the Eames? Some inkling of the answer is to be found in this book. It is the fruit of eight years' work by Ray Eames and her collaborators, to celebrate her husband's achievements, at the end of which she herself died, ten years to the day since Charles' death. Despite the elegant design of the book, it comes over as an obsessive document, relying on minute point sizes on a large page to cram in information, and documenting relentlessly each and every project the couple had shared. It is a complete catalogue, without criticism or commentary other than factual background.

This approach raises two questions: why does such a documentation exist (and is it sufficient) and what was the real degree of collaboration between the Eames. Ray was rarely present at client meetings, though she became the mental archivist of the office, and was almost always consulted on choices of colour and materials (she had studied weaving at Cranbrook). Comments from those who worked for the couple insist on their obsessive requirement to record and document any and everything. (Ralph Caplan had a summer job as a student working as a photographer for the Eames, capturing every meeting and greeting.) Their archive was donated to the Library of Congress, with the support of a grant from IBM: after several truckloads of material arrived in Washington, the Library discreetly let in be known that in the event of future donations by other designers a certain amount of advance winnowing would be preferred.

It seems to me that the Eames were the first designers in post-war America to realise the nature of publicity and the image of the designer. Unlike Raymond Loewy, who wanted to be on the cover of *Time* magazine to be the equal of the business magnates who were his clients, the Eames understood, almost intuitively, that one could be famous for being special. And their talents were discovered at a time when there was opportunity and resources in plenty. California in the 1940s and early 1950s had been transformed by the war industries and then by postwar investment in research (much of it funded by the military.) Nowhere else in the world at the time could even a rich man such as John Entenza, owner of *Arts & Architecture*, build a few 'case study houses', just for a magazine feature. The Eames came to represent a certain California lifestyle, free, colourful and creative, separate from the left-wing implications of Berkeley and other campuses.

Their success meant they could select the projects they preferred, and indulge their interest in subjects such as the circus, American history, and the power of mathematics. These choices are in themselves a reflection of the new, science-based and vibrant vision of the American way. This new way was separated by the width of a continent from the old coal and steel industries of the East coast, and so was the ideal vehicle for the relaunch of a new image of America. An image which the Eames' exhibitions and films came increasingly to support and so represent. The Eames offered a paradigm of successful, all-American design. No wonder everyone, of a certain generation, wanted to be like them.

Ranting for Real

Victor Papanek
DESIGN FOR THE REAL WORLD
Thames & Hudson, London, 1972

There is a welsh word, *hwyl*, used to descrkibe the state of performance of a nonconformist preacher, halfway into his sermon, afire with holy wrath, with another forty minutes to go, and deep into the rhetorics of hellfire and damnation. The English translation might be 'rantery', if such a noun for ranting existed, but that would miss the point. Ranting is seen as a negative activity, while 'having the hwyl' is a compliment: it suggests determination, skill and a certain integrity, even if of a fundamentalist sort.

Papanek's Design for the Real World is a rant, but it has a certain hwyl to it, as well. A rant – now, for reasons we might look at later, an unfashionable form of discourse – requires certain basics. The first is an inflexible moral position from which to attack whatever targets the speaker has in mind. The second is a rhetorical use of language to steamroller any logical objections to the argument, and the third is purpose, in the sense that the rant is not merely against the failings of society, but also proposes, often as blindingly obvious, remedies and solutions for those failings. A ranter does not just fulminate against the evils of his day – as the bigot does – but also offers an alternative. This is an important distinction: someone who attacks the present with no view of the future can be left to simmer, but a skewed view of the future demands a reply.

Papanek's central argument is that designers have become the willing slaves of crass capitalism, only apt to do the bidding of their white, male, middle-class masters and so excluding from the benefits of technology females, coloureds, the poor and non-Americans. This analysis is delivered with gusto and a degree of wit (the description of a blow-up female doll as 'looking unnervingly like Jacqueline Kennedy Onassis' is a masterly touch, to take just one example.) And given that Papanek's subject matter is American design of the 1950s and 1960s (the book was published in 1972) he is not lost for absurdities and excesses to castigate. But his argument, whatever its merits, is tripped up by his own enthusiasm. The definition of design itself is a chameleon, changing its connotation to fit the twists of his tirades. Design, he suggests, should not be considered as beautiful or good, but meaningful: but meaning full of what is not clear. Craft objects, corporate commissions, individual designer products and anonymous manufacturers' goods all fall pell-mell under the same whiplash. This deliberate confusion is reinforced by rhetorical devices: 'books of trash' (a favourite word, but undefined) are compared with 'volumes' of quality, even when both emanate from the same publishers. Syllogisms are common (products in one market are not rigorously tested, tested products are inadequate, therefore all products are failures.) False statistics are another ploy (only 5 out of 501 designs approved by the Museum of Modern Art in New York went into production, therefore MoMA is failing in its role as arbiter of design, etc.)

Papanek's solution is for designers to become the agents of change on behalf of the people, rather than the lackeys of industry. Designers must accept their moral and social responsibility, and work for (or preferably in) the Third World, and design for the oppressed, the poor, for children, for the disabled, for pregnant women. He provides a raft of examples – mainly drawn from the work of his students at Purdue University – as to how such design can be achieved, can do better and cost less than commercial solutions. As a first step towards this, he suggests design companies put a percentage of their creative energy and budget to such causes. But at to the refabrication of the socio-ecomonic nexus within which contemporary design exists and operates, as implied in his argument, he offers no solution.

Papanek's book enjoyed a considerable succes d'estime when it appeared, and it is still widely cited. His positive argument that designers have a social obligation as well as a client obligation would not raise a murmur of protest today. And, from today's standpoint, it is easy to sympathise with his evident anger at the meretricious nature of much American design of the 1960s. So should we forgive Papanek his excessive arguments, because he gets some answers right? No.

No because bad arguments do not validate correct answers, and no because even from an 1972 standpoint Papanek's position is a wrong one. For all his valuable comments, Papanek cannot escape from his view that the American hegemony is necessary, that American values matter, that American capitalism is the only real model. The notion that there are other design traditions, in Europe or in Japan, for example, or other social conventions than crass market forces, escapes him completely. The simplicities of the Cold War find an unexpected but endless echo throughout his text. His description of consumers as ignorant, duped and dumb is as offensive – and unrealistic – as his portrayal of management as simply greedy and designers as serfs. This top-down model recurs in one of his favourite projects, a free television service for Africa. Local carpenters would create insect proof cases for the cathode ray tubes provided by (suddenly benevolent) television manufacturers, but the sets would be programmed to receive only one channel, provided by UNESCO. The idea that Africans might have something to say to other Africans does not get a peek over Big Brother's shoulder. Papanek himself may have been unaware of how his own words were couched in the sterile rhetoric of the Cold War, but his simplistic analysis of the relationship between designer, products and society and his failure to understand the nature of consumption make his search for a design utopia not merely irrelevant but ludicrous.

Cool Collage

Marshall McLuhan & Quentin Fiore
The Medium is the Massage
Penguin Books, Harmondsworth, 1967

A Penguin book with integrated pictures in it, in 1967?
Heresy, or what? Penguin Books, founded by Allen Lane
just before the Second World War, is a story of good luck
and good judgement. Good luck in that when book printing paper was rationed at the beginning of the war, quo-
tas were based on 1938/9 production levels per publishing
house, and Penguin, with a large programme of mass publishing, did very well from that, and good judgement in
that Lane maintained a balanced list through and after the
war, and so established Penguin as a serious general publisher, as well as persuading book buyers to buy paperback editions. His editorial judgement was solid if a little
conservative: the only error he made was to refuse, after
the war, to publish war memoirs or war fiction, an un-
dersatandable decision, perhaps, but one which was to give
other, competing imprints a clear run at a large part of
the market in the 1950s and 1960s. Lane believed in product quality, and so invited Jan Tschichold, a distinguished
Swiss typographer, to redesign the logo and the identity of
the list in the late 1940s. Tschichold established clear branding for the different categories, as well as improving the
overall visual appearance. Green was used as a base colour for detective fiction, orange for fiction, blue for
Pelican non-fiction, for example. The Penguin offer was
clear, ordered and authoritative. So what was this book of
pictures doing in an orange wrapper?

Not just pictures in the sense of halftones on gloss art
paper with white borders and informative captions, as in
Pelican books, but fully bled details, with type over them,

on a matt stock. And typography that wouch change size
as you turned the page, even when continuing the same
sentence. What was this? It was 'an inventory of effects'
(the book's subtitle) created by McLuhan and Fiore to celebrate and demonstrate McLuhan's popular and controver-
sial ideas about media and technology, and their role in
contemporary society. McLuhan was a Canadian academic, who ran the University of Toronto's Center for Culture
and Tecnhology from 1944 till his retirement in 1977 (he
died in 1980.) He published a number of formal books,
including *Understsanding Media*, *The Gutenberg Galaxay*
and *War and Peace in the Global Village*. Hisd central
concept was that all technologies represent extensions of
the human body, and as such change our perceptions of
our environment and our sensory world. The car as an
extension of the foot, the book as an extension of the eye,
and, most importantly, electronic communication (television, telephony and computing) as an extension of the central nervous system. These changes of perception, he insisted, result from the existence of the media themselves,
not from their content. The fundamental change of the
twentieth century, he argued, was the end of the Gutenberg era, the end of the dominance of linearly directed,
information rich, low entrope printed matter as a primary means of communication, and the arrival of new media
which have overturned the past totally. Our relationship
with time and space, our distinctions between public and
private, have been radically and inevitably altered: 'print
technology created the public. Electric technology created
the mass. The public consists of separate individuals walking around with separate, fixed points of viewe. the new
technology demands that we abandon the luxury of this
posture, this fragmentary outlook'. We now live in 'a global village', and have to reinvent ways of communication
and expression that use the new media. His work set out
to chart these changes, and did so with vigour and wit,
and not a little anger.

For, he argued, and this is one of the main premises of *The Medium is the Massage*, our institutions have not ad-aprted to this change, and existing power structures, their authority based in the old media, have no desire to change at all: 'our official culture is striving to force the new media to do the work of the old', as he says, placing the words over a still from Bergman's film *The Seventh Seal*, an image that itself echoes the mediaeval dance of death. The book is a call to arms, a demand for new policies in education and new systems in government. The book's message is reinforced by its format and design – early monochrome multimedia, and by the subtle comparison of imagery and text. It was unlike anything before: no wonder Penguin, though they knew thay had to have it, didn't know where in their ordered, Gutenberg-dominated list, to put it.

McLuhan gave the radicals of the 1960s a whole armoury of arguments for change, and protest. The way in which television imagery of the Vietnam war changed American's perceptions of the rightness of the war has often been cited, and justifies McLuhan's position. The revolution in interactive media today can also be seen in McLuhanesque terms: we saw the Tianammen Square massacre and the bombing of Serbia live, in real time, on the global village square of the television screen. No-one doubts his underlying thesis that changes on communication technology, in particular, change cultures, and that we are living through a period of technologically-driven radical change. McLuhan charted those changes with vigourous historical examples and telling one-liners, but he failed to understand the ability of economic forces to adapt to change, and his rigid categorisation of media into hot and cold, quite apart from being confusing at a time when everyone wanted to be simply cool, undervalued the role of content. Today, while we might be wired in ways in which he never imagined, we are still not connected.

Final Frontiersmen

Tom Wolfe
THE RIGHT STUFF
Simon & Schuster, New York, 1986

The story goes that Reagan, in his last starring role as
President of the USA, was chatting to Gorbachev after one
of their meetings on detente. 'I wonder', Reagan asked,
'what would have happened if instead of Kennedy it had
been Kruschev who had been assassinated?' Tovarich
Mikhail paused for some time before replying. 'I think'.
he finally said, 'that Aristotle Onasssis would not have
married Mrs Kruschev'. Gorbachev, though he failed later
to impose his vision, clearly had a better understanding of
history (and a fine wit, if there is any truth to the story,
which there almost certainly is not.)

But Reagan's question, real or not, conceals a real and
deep fear: what if the USA had lost (whether or not the
'evil empire' thereby won.) Would a world order in which
American hegemony was not supreme be possible: was it
even a thinkable proposition (even after decades of thinking the unthinkable in terms of nuclear megadeaths)? Tom
Wolfe's *The Right Stuff* is ostensibly a reconstruction of
the background to the Mercury spaceflights that put Americans into space for the first time, but it is in fact an analysis of the horror vacui that American failure – at whatever level – might entail. And it becomes an enquiry into
the nature of failure and the concomitant impossibility of
success.

Wolfe achieves this firstly by linking the story of the Mercury missions with earlier manned high-atmosphere flight
tests, particularly the series of tests into rocket-propelled
aircraft run from Edwardes Airforce Base in California in
the early 1950s, when Chuck Yeager became the first

person to fly beyond the speed of sound. Many of the Mercury team came from this cardre of test pilots, but Wolfe interest in them is as an elite group, the top of the invisible ziggurat of pilot achievement. In this sense, the battles between the Mercury astronauts and NASA about whether the astronauts would fly as pilots or passengers was crucial to the astronauts' own sense of self-worth among their peers. For Wolfe, small. isolated groups, often male, have often been a focus: his early articles, in which he created what was termed 'the New Journalism', both for its subject matter and its use of language, often dealt with such groups: custom car makers, stock-car racing drivers and so forth. It sometimes seems as if, for Wolfe, such groups, often on the frontiers of society, represent a certain essential Americanness. Lose them, he seems to be saying, and America loses too. Other Americans have shared such a view: the English critic Peter Wollen (*Signs and Meaning in the Cinema*, 1969) has argued that many of Howard Hawks' films can be read as stories of elite, marginalised groups of men, and that this is as potent an American myth as the wilderness/civilisation dichotomy in, for example, the films of John Ford. Norman Mailer's first novel, *The Naked and the Dead*, an ironic account of men at war, also proposes the importance of the closed group with its own code. One could extend this argument to suggest that the dark shadows over Wolfe's first novel, *The Bonfire of the Vanities*, stems from the loss of this quality in his characters.

The second thread Wolfe uses is the atmosphere of hysteria bordering on panic that the initial Russian successes with Sputnik, the first earth-orbit satellite, and with Gagarin's mission, the first manned space flight, created in the American public, and in political and military leaders. The idea that the Soviets were ahead in the technology race led to the space race, and put the Mercury astronauts into the front line, idolised by the American media and treated as heroes by the public. Wolfe's coruscating prose style brings this very much to life. More importantly, he shows how the group adjusted to their new public role, creating for themselves an American vision that they shared with their public. But in the process they compromised or moved away from the values of their peer grouip, the other possessors of 'the right stuff', an unspoken quality of balance, fearlessness and preparedness that is beyond mere courage or skill. The fragmentation of the core values of the group under outside pressure is, for Wolfe, tragic: and also ironic, in that the fragmentation came at a time when the members of the group were being hailed as the saviours of everything American. The Mercury missions were one of the first truly mediated political and scientific events of our time, one of the occasions that were brought into the home of the people by television, as well as being devloped before by extensive press coverage. But putting the frontiersmen in front of the cameras destroyed the myth. Wolfe attempts to salvage this by returning to Chuck Yeager at the end of the book, to show how while everything else has changed in aerospace, the guy with 'the right stuff' is still hanging in there. But while it makes an elegant coda to the story, it does not ring true: we know that the race into space broke up the brotherhood, and thanks to the power of Wolfe's writing we share, for a moment, his sense of loss.

The strength of this book lies in the convincing portrait it offers of America, and parts of American society, at one of the high points in the American hegemony, at a time when technology and resources, and so ambition, were seen as limitless. America could, it bel;ieved, create anything, design anything. Wolfe brings to his subject a passion he clearly felt, and so offers an enthralling vision of the limitations of success, and the place of America in the world, just before the Kennedy assassination, and the war in Vietnam shattered the dream.

Frivolous Europe

Household Gods

EMILIO AMBASZ (EDITOR)
ITALY: THE NEW DOMESTIC LANDSCAPE
Achievements and Problems of Italian Design.
MoMA New York, 1972

Anyone old enough to remember inflatable furniture will find this book an immediate nostalgia fix. (I was once stopped from boarding a bus because my Olivetti Valentine – my first design icon – was considered to be a can full of petrol.) The very names of the design groups – Archizoom and Superstudio – are redolent of the time, and the dynamic graphics for Joe Colombo's furniture or Alberto Rosselli's projected living spaces, or of Gruppo Strum's photo-romances on the future of the city recall the enthusiasms and causes of the late 1960s: the formal invitation to Enzo Mari NOT to design an environment – and his acceptance of it over three pages – says it all.

But beneath these glowing acrylic freeform shapes lies a serious statement of purpose. The exhibition for which this is the catalogue confirmed, through the Museum of Modern Art's imprimatur, the post-war supremacy of Italian design for living. This was in part thanks to the encouragement of companies such as Olivetti and Fiat, and in part to the parallel contribution of the port-war Italian film industry, whether through the enigmatic ordinary life of Antonioni, the distorted parables of Pasolini or the gargantuan extravaganzas of Fellini. Magazines, small exhibitions (Olivetti's Concept and Form exhibition had just finished a world tour) and a few books had already spread the word: this was the endorsement. The exhibition was put together in under a year, with the drama, emotion and extempore panic that flavours the best Italian creativity. But there was a real determination to maintain and develop Italy's poll position. That part of the programme continues to succeed, long after the inflatable furniture has gone down and the hype has blown over.

The Milan Salone, the annual furniture fair, has launched the careers of many designers – Italian and other – and all Italian industry, *tangentopoli* or not, continues to endorse good design values as almost a reflex action. Take the 1995 Fiat Coupe, a deservedly award-winning design. Over the wheel arches there are dramatic slashes in the bodywork, that give an instant impression of style and speed, like a signature. On the production vehicle they look as sharp and bright as they must have done on the first clay model. No other motor manufacturer would have carried such a design endorsement all the way through, at that time or earlier (compare the similar but fudged marks on a Triumph TR7, for example.) For product and furniture design, Italian work can rarely be faulted for its lack of design input. The same is not true of Italian graphics, a reflection of an educational system that – unlike other European models – promoted architecture over two-dimensional design. The result is a thriving design culture that in an age of product globalization, still gives Italian work its own character and *brio*, just as the authors and creators in this catalogue predicted.

Archizoom chair, 1969

Milano, Milano

ALBRECHT BANGERT
ITALIAN FURNITURE DESIGN
Translation by Lucas Dietrich
Bangert Verlag, Munich 1992

'Italian furniture design has never suffered from conformity or a shortage of ideas' Albrecht Bangert points out midway through his 1985 book, *Italian Furniture Design*. It is a statement hardly in doubt by then, after the designs of Carlo Molino and Gaetano Pesce, the UB series of gigantic feet and books, or the gaudy blowups of D'Urbino, Lomazzi and De Pas. And fifteen years after the book was pub lished, and despite the economic vagaries of the late 1980s, Italian furniture design is still vigorous – even if the mix of designers working in and around Milan is now less exclusively Italian than it was, say, at the time of the *New Domestic Landscape* exhibition in 1972.

Bangert offers several reasons for the post-war success and later supremacy of Italian furniture design. One is the ex-

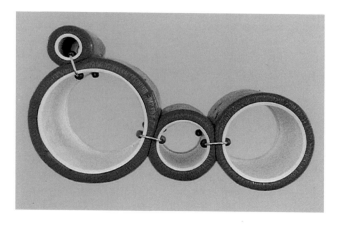

istence of an infrastructure of craftsmanship which may have been muted under Mussolini but was never destroyed by capitalist mass industry: rather the uniquely Italian concept of the *fabbrica* combined craft skills with short-run production techniques and an independent-minded openness to new ideas that other models of craft production (notably the Anglo-Saxon one) cannot encompass. Secondly he cites an architectural education system that actively involved architects in interior, furniture and product design, without constraining its students to hierarchise architectural models only. And thirdly, a need to redefine the cultural values of the country in a new way after the disaster of Fascism.

The success of industrial reconstruction in Germany and Japan after the physical catastrophe of World War II is well-known, while the question of cultural regeneration and redefinition has been less closely watched, partly because, I expect, of the need to maintain both countries as frontiers against Communism. Italy, less scarred physically by the war, began a more visual programme of regenerating its culture, through film and literature as well as through design. But there is a deeper historical reason, in my own view, for the way in which design has become

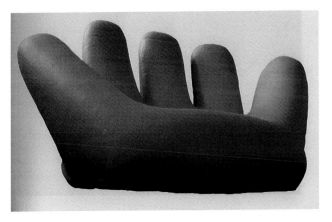

part of social and business culture in Italy in ways it has never achieved elsewhere. The idea of the artist as the independent creator, moved by his or her own gods and muses, detached, in that respect, from contemporary society, is a largely English and American one, and not one shared by the rest of Europe. That their artists or writers might be spiritually richer, and more capable of artistic expression, that certainly, but that they were a race apart – certainly not. The notion of the Romantic artist is an inherently nineteenth century one (and like most nineteenth century ideas, inherently wrong..) It sprang from the inability of a class system such as the English Victorian one to put creativity (or intellectual ability of any kind) into a suitable pigeonhole: it was easier to deny its existence. This had not been a problem in the past: no-one worried about Samuel Johnson or Dean Swift's lack of birth, for example (and even the aristocracy were more worried about their ideas than their parentage.)

In Italy the place of the architect and designer (and most designers were also architects) in society was not uncertain or doubtful; the radical ideas of the young might worry their elders, as between many generations, but in general the designer recognised the ability of the craftsman, the craftsman the quality of the designer and the client the skill and integrity of both- that had been true from the Renaissance if not even before. *Eppur si muove*, as Galileo is supposed to have said after his recantation: the centre still holds.

Previous pages: left, Tubo armchair by Joe Colombo, 1969, right, Joe seating by Lomazzi, D'Urbino and De Pas, 1970.

Petit Bourgeois Dreams

ROLAND BARTHES
MYTHOLOGIES
Translated by Anne Lavers
Paladin, London, 1972
(Original edition, Le Seuil, Paris, 1957)

This little book of essays by the French hero of the new criticism has been continuously in print since it was translated into English in 1972. Its semiological analysis of everyday events – among them wrestling, steak and chips, soap powders, lawsuits and wine – was original, witty and profound, opening up new ways of appreciating and understanding social and cultural activity. By deconstructing the myths of the petit bourgeoisie so fluently, Barthes in fact fashioned a tool for generations of advertising executives, who did not always deploy his models with the same acuity or wit.

Barthes's method, analysed in the final section of the book, is to analyse not the apparent content of a subject, but its symbolism. For him the everyday objects or events he discusses all carry several layers of meaning, in a stepped pattern of *signe, signifiant* and *signifié* with the *signe* at the base level modulated by language and myth: by myth he means a secondary semiological system, that adds further value, through history, culture and knowledge. This mythic content changes as culture changes, and to understand the   significance of everyday objects we need to understand everyday culture. And in addition we need to understand the role of the media (in particular the illustrated press, the most powerful medium at the time he was writing) in promoting a particular set of cultural values, often those of the petit-bourgeoisie, with its narrow self interest.

In an appropriately mythic way, the book does not only seek to analyse scientifically the phenomenon and explain the semiological process, it also seeks to expose the political bias of the French media and a number of French institutions.

Take for example the essay on flying saucers (not included, along with several others, mainly on French political issues such as Poujadisme, in the English edition.) Barthes is not interested in whether they exist or not: people believe they exist; that is what matters, and his questions are about the nature of this belief and its implications. At first, he says, people thought they came from the Soviet Union, a country itself of myth and mystery, where anything was possible. Later their source became Mars, as attributing so much power to the Soviets was uncomfortable. And so the myth changed; vehicles for warriors became agents of justice. Faced with interplanetary punishment, the Cold War looks embarrassing. But what does this tell us about Martians? Barthes points out that for the petit bourgeois mentality, the concept of radical otherness is not possible. Martians must, therefore, be like us, have a society and history like ours. As he points out, one Lyon newspaper went so far as to assert that the Martians must be monotheists, and probably had a Pope as well! Barthes comments that on this basis if we ever got to Mars we wouldn't recognise the difference. But the serious point is that by placing the Martians (whom we hope are like ourselves) above the world, in the sky, in judgement, the petit bourgeois mentality subliminates its fear of destruction by the atomic bomb into a mythical ally. (Tim Burton's film, *Mars Attacks*, shows indeed that Martians are just like some of us – violent, devious and hating bad music.)

For designers, the essay on 'The New Citroen' (the 1955 Citroen DS 19) is the great paean to product design – 'the supreme creation of an era, conceived with passion... and consumed in image if not in usage by a whole population... as a purely magical object'. He points out that the vehicle was displayed at the Paris Motor Show without wheels: and that in the myth wheels were redundant. 'We are therefore dealing here with a humanized art, and it is possible that the *Déesse* marks a change in the mythology of cars. Until now, the ultimate in cars belonged rather to the bestiary of power; here it becomes at once more spiritual and more object-like.' The Citroen logo is also part of this change: 'the Citroen emblem, with its arrows, has in fact become a winged emblem, as if one was proceeding from the category of propulsion to that of spontaneous motion, from that of the engine to that of the organism'.

By apparently validating design activity in terms of social expression, Barthes joined McLuhan as an early intellectual guru of design, even if much of his later thinking was not absorbed by designers – perhaps thanks to the denseness of the writing, not of the readers.

This book underscores Barthes's ability as a writer : as one of his biographers has pointed out, Barthes did not have a normal academic career, instead working as a freelance writer and critic for several years, a time which honed his writing skills. His influence as a critic is undoubted. The irony that he brings to the humdrum – pre-*Mythologies* humdrum, that is – is no less strong for being applied with charm and at times with real humour (the idea of Robbe-Grillet's novel *Le Voyeur* as a prize in a striptease competition, for example). We never looked at a margarine advert in the same way again.

The Logics of Magic

ETTORE SOTTSASS, JNR.
DESIGNING DREAMS
Idea Books, Milan, 1987

Ettore Sottsass's birthplace, in north-eastern Italy, is on one of the hinges of European culture, where Latin and Teuton meet. A post-hoc rationalisation could then explain the logic and magic of Sottsass's work as a designer in terms of such influences. The truth is considerably more complex and more subtle.

Sottsass trained as an architect in Turin during the Fascist epoch, when a plan to create 'the most modern street in Europe' in glass and steel was rejected for political reasons in favour of traditional solution (Mussolini himself resolved one debate over architectural style by declaring that since the Romans had invented the arch, it was the only proper way to build in Italy.) After qualifying, he worked briefly as a designer for Fiat (probably the first designer they employed as such,) before being drafted into the Italian army and sent to Yugoslavia, where he was captured and spent the rest of the war in a prison camp.

He came back to an Italy that had been, in his view, defeated and depleted. This is a view that can perhaps be questioned, in absolute terms: Italy had not suffered the physical destruction inflicted on Germany and Japan, nor had the repression of the intelligentsia under Mussolini been anything like as extreme as in Germany. But from an Italian viewpoint, the situation was still a sorry one. With courage and passion Sottsass began working as an independent architect and designer, entering competitions for housing projects, and making prototypes for furniture and lamps. His talent was soon noticed by a number of companies, including Olivetti, who have employed him as a freelance consultant almost continuously ever since. His early work for Olivetti is characterised by its humanity of form: the most famous design is probably the bright red Valentine typewriter, the first bit of office equipment chic enough to carry in the street.

Sottsass's political awareness began in the 1930s. 'Italian design started,' he once said, 'with the idea that designing is a political – and moral – event, in the sense of confronting oneself with society, history and the anthropological state of the tribe.' He was involved with various design associations and groups looking to redefine design outside its traditional and bourgeois framework, that were active in Italy in the 1960s and 1970s. The most famous group of them all was Memphis, in which he played a leading role. Memphis's redefinition of design through powerful colour and asymmetrical form was a radical and ludic event that still echoes through the world of design, even though the first Memphis show was in 1981. Memphis emphasised the role of play and surprise in the role of even the most conventional design, insisting on design's key role in establishing the visionary and ritualistic qualities of everyday life.

It is to this metaphorical view of design, design as the activity of homo ludens, that this book of drawings, photographs, poems and occasional writing refers. What Sottsass called 'the devising of stage sets for the happy, sad, romantic, cynical, public and private stories and characters that represent the endless episodes of the dramatic story of life.' Together the different elements form a fragmentary but inspiring record of a lifetime spent devoted to uncovering and enjoying the mystery and pleasure of existence. It has both everything and nothing to do with the formal work Sottsass does as a designer.

Designing the Designer

PHILPPE STARCK
STARCK
Taschen Verlag, Cologne and London, 1996

The designer looks out from the cover, his nude torso fetchingly adorned with drawings of his own works, the Olympic Flame over his right kidney, Juicy Salif over the breastbone, the Aprilia Moto roaring towards his belly-button. It is an image both ludicrous and curious, down to the mocking body-builder pose and the ironic, slightly apologetic look in the designer's eyes. This could only be Starck, is one's first realisation. No-one else could achieve the same anatopism, or present themselves in quite that way, arrogant yet somehow modest, saying I did this/ this was done.

Inside the book the reader finds an endless gallery of images, laid to a stark and fully-bled grid, with occasional

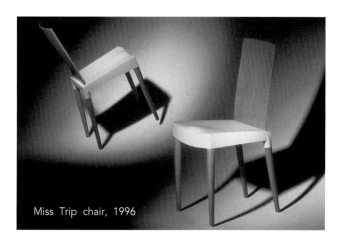

Miss Trip chair, 1996

simple exhortations 'Pax now' set against a photograph of Starck's face in stitches after a bike accident, 'Le Civisme est d'avant-garde' (Starck in a suit of armour), 'Nous sommes Dieu' (Starck with megaphone on head, like a dunce's cap.) The other photographs of interiors, furniture, industrial design, projects and architecture are intercut with images of Starck family and friends, what he calls his 'tribe'. Captions are at a minimum, often just the name of the product and its date: many pictures have no explanation at all. The quality of the photography, design and print is excellent, making reading by looking itself a pleasure. At the end, three short interviews with different journalists, dealing with Starck's current preoccupations and thinking. Over the endpapers, a list of homages: Mendelsohn and Gaudi, Lynch and Wenders, Calder and Chareau, Mendini and Scarpa.

Those who glibly think of Starck as the egotist par excellence will find much in this book to justify such a superficial view. But Starck is not a media animal: he doesn't talk to the press that often, doesn't appear on TV, doesn't go to parties or appear on the social pages of magazines and newspapers. Meeting him, he is both conscious of and astonished by his success, willing to talk about the future but not to explain the past. For Starck, his work stands for itself, not for him. He is not a personality, rather a *persona* – the Latin word means mask, and its transliteration into French, as Michel Tournier has pointed out, means both an individual person and the absence of any person. What he presents in this book – an astonishing body of work for some twenty five years' activity – could be entitled 'what has been done' as much as 'what I have done.' There is no celebration here of how Starck has achieved all this, rather an insistence, underlined by the formal visual design of the book itself, that all this needed to be done. This approach is explained by the texts at the end, setting out – in oblique and Starckian fashion – his ideas on the duty of designers and the necessity of design. Just as his naked torso on the cover becomes a costume for his favourite designs, so the images of Starck and his family and friends that punctuate the book are not there to say to the reader 'look what we did' rather 'think about how and why.'

This modest message is delivered, of course, with glee, bravura and wit. Not to confuse the reader but to amuse, to drive the delight through the pages to the end, where, as in the best stories, some but not all is revealed (just as some but not all was revealed on the cover.) The book holds up a mirror to the creative process, and through its design (excellently crafted by Mark Thomson) it sets a new benchmark as to how books on design should present and celebrate the complex but real mysteries of the craft.

Taschen published their first book on Starck in 1988, just as their innovative approach to marketing books was breaking up the dozy chumminess of British bookselling. Their approach was based on bulk advance selling, zero warehoused stock, and competitive American-style discounts. They were seen at first as competitors for the remainder book market, something similar to the successful promotional book publishers in the USA. But Taschen offered new material, not reprints, and production values and design qualities that were the equivalent, if not better than, contemporary first publishing practice. The Taschen revolution has made immense differences to the book trade (along with a range of other wider economic factors.) Their first book on Starck had a thin and lightweight text, and a wholly conventional structure. It is a mark of the distance that both Starck and his publishers have gone in the interval that this book's authoritative dismissal of convention seems so right and so convincing.

Living the Techno-Life

PETER COOK & OTHERS
A GUIDE TO ARCHIGRAM 1961 – 74
Academy Editions, London

Archigram returns! The plug-in, tune-up, see-through group from the 1960s and early 1970s are compactly celebrated in a new book of texts and commentaries. The wall posters, all Cow Gum and Letraset, the collages of Twiggy and Superman, are here too, for Archigram's mission to explain always took a visual form. Some of the Pop glamour is lost, as the images are squeezed down on to CD – sized pages, though bulking out to the size of a boxed set of Siegfried and Gotterdammerung.

Just as Wagner tried to create a new bourgeois mythology for nineteenth century Germany, so Archigram set out a radical new agenda for the 1960s. Theirs was to be a world in which everything was electrical, disposable, portable, consumable. Every mention was a manifesto, every competition a call to arms. Chalk, Herron, Cook, Crompton, Greene and Webb cut a swathe through the architectural schools of the time, leaving the Modernists green with anger and their students giddy with delight. As a remedy for the cold, gray, Cold War world of the 1950s Archigram was wonderful: all colour, provocation and Zoom T-shirts.

But it was only a cold remedy, not a cure. The endless fizz of ideas has no core programme that would outlast the exclamation marks. Archigram became trapped inside the plug-in bubble of their own vision, which led on to endless variations on the same themes, but only rarely to finished buildings. But because of the well-known low ability of the English to distinguish genres, Archigram are termed architects rather than designers or theorists: but architects create buildings, designers design them – and stop there. Yet even as radical theorists Archigram became caught up in their own rhetoric. A lot of their proposals raise, but failed to answer, other questions – particularly about the use of materials and the consumption of energy – that were conveniently ignored, along with the social implications of their proposed world of individual living pots. Take two of their most bizarre proposals, the Rokplug and Logplug. Cunningly disguised as part of the natural landscape, these were actually plug-in terminals for phone, television, and, oddly, water. Apart from the kitsch – almost Victorian – design connotations of this idea, reminiscent of gaslamps disguised as sunflowers from the Great Exhibition, no consideration was given to the environmental impact of channelling in all these services.

Essentially Archigram failed to understand the ways in which technology was moving around them. Ivan Sutherland's article 'The ultimate display' that set the agenda for virtual reality was published in 1965, by which time the first ARPA network was already running. Miniaturisation was about to create the PC and later the portable phone. Today any rock or log will to do to sit on to use a Powerbook.

This was not merely a wrong guess: Archigram were obsessed with the power structures of connected hardware. That it is in fact software that creates choices, that empowers the user, was an argument that passed them by. (This despite the debate going on in parallel, in magazines such as Control and Ark). The radical ferment stirred up by Archigram stimulated many students, and provoked a debate that cleared some of the stuffiness of Modernism from the air. But the ferment never distilled. Archigram remained lost in their plastic fishtank, plugged into an outdated and greedy technology.

The True Blue Brits

PETER YORK & ANN BARR
THE OFFICIAL SLOANE RANGER HANDBOOK
Ebury Press, London, 1982

The enormous and almost spontaneous public grief at the death of Diana Princess of Wales in a car accident in 1997 was a worldwide phenomenon: it was stimulated by the media (for whom the Princess had been the source of endless copy over the years) and among the many things it masked was the very different circumstances in which she had got married some twenty years before. The wedding was promoted as the event of the century, a fairy-tale performance: one major American television station in fact ran their main evening news program from a portable studio in front of Buckingham Palace in the run-up to the big event. It was, the hype said, the beginning of a new era (rather as the groom's mother's accession to the throne in 1952 had been hailed as the start of the 'new Elizabethan age.') And who were to be the beneficiaries of this great social upheaval?

Not surprisingly, the general answer is the urban middle classes, who have reaped the main benefits from most social changes in English history. But Charles and Diana's wedding was also seen as validating the status of a narrower group within the urban middle class, the London-based upper middle class, especially those with the right educational background, social connections and lifestyle. This group is the subject of Peter York and Anne Barr's 1982 *The Official Sloane Ranger Handbook.*

The Sloane Ranger is a punning title for the young people living around Sloane Square in central London, a fashionable, respectable and expensive area. The Handbook offers in solemn form a guide to their plumage (Husky coats and green wellies), habitat (Fulham Road if need be, but never south of the River Thames), pecking order (landed gentry and Guards officers to the fore), feeding habits (salmon mousse to cod-in-a-bag), songs and calls (Hooray Henries here), courtship and mating rituals (Hunt Balls and the Admiral Codrington pub), migratory patterns (skiing), nesting and rearing young (getting the ratling's name down for a good school.) This analysis of a strange species is delivered with gusto, using the characters of Henry and Caroline as models. 'The Sloane life looks comfortable and reassuring. Good manners, nursery food, the same shirts for five years. It must be right, mustn't it?... The Sloane's style, the eternal stream of English life, an invaluable reference for a lifetime of decisions about What Really Matters in life. You can't go wrong.'

The anthropological analysis of this tribe, its empty heads full of certainties and simple but silly rules ('French bread and rolls: break with the fingers, never cut with a knife') is accompanied by detailed lists of where to shop for what, where to live, and which schools, universities, jobs, ski resorts, reading matter ('anyone who has read Proust is not a Sloane') are approved, and so on. The irony here is that, unlike its American counterpart, the Preppies Handbook, buying the right kit (and even learning the soppy slang) does not make you a Sloane. Sloanes, as the authors point out, are born not made: at best you could use the book as a guide to breeding (if not in-breeding) one. The humour of all this is delightful, in a rather English way, with a sufficient degree of deliberate absurdity to relate it to the traditions if not of the Goon Show at least of the Glums.

But what is unfunny about it is that Sloanery created a social model that substituted status for values, preferred the interests of their group to that of the wider community, and enjoyed a sphere of influence considerably larger than their numbers or intellectual capacities entitled them to. Of course it is in the nature of social groups to seek to gain and retain power, but what is pernicious about the right wing in England is its lack of any intellectual argument, and reliance on precedent, tradition, class loyalty and nationalism instead. Thus the resistance to innovation in architecture and design, the insistence on conservation and heritage at the expense of invention, that has been a hallmark of English reaction to opportunities to be creative for the last fifty years, a reaction strengthened by the two decades of Thatcherism, with its unparalleled cuts in arts funding, education and public works investment.

A moment's comparison with France and Germany over the same period shows just how pitiful this cultural vision was, with its appeal to 'Victorian values,' to simplistic ideas of honest thrift and entrepreneurship. But the true values of the Victorian age were fear of the future and moral hypocrisy, that would allow child labour and teenage prostitution to flourish while invoking the name of God to stifle debate. The irony is that the economic revolution under Thatcher destroyed the safe base of jobs in the City of London for Sloanes, and let property speculation rip through their cherished parts of London. Seen today, York's book is a guide to an endangered species. And not all endangered species are worth saving.

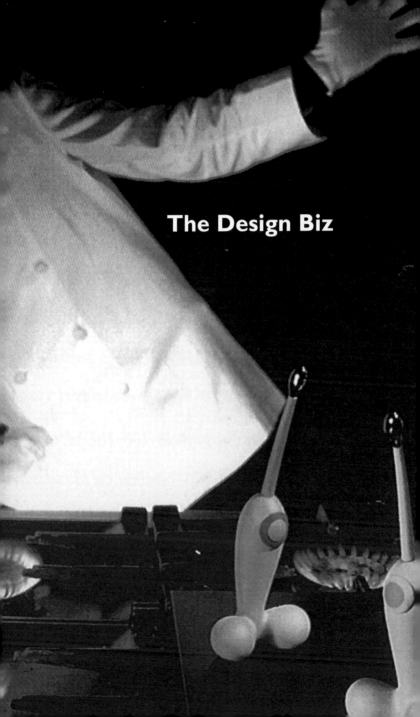

The Design Biz

American Wisdoms

RALPH CAPLAN
BY DESIGN
McGraw Hill, New York, 1982

I once met Ralph Caplan in the offices he used in the Herman Miller building in downtown New York. We had been discussing the role of design management (then very much a buzz-word). 'I agree about its importance', he said finally, walking over to the window, 'but, look, no-one ever told them!' And he pointed to the jumble of signage, advertising, and information graphics that makes up an average New York street. Caplan has been navigating this visual sprawl (William Gibson called his future New York urban complex The Sprawl) for many years, as a consultant to Hermann Miller, and as the author of a regular column in ID magazine in New York, where he was also editor, as well as chairing for several years the Aspen Design Conference. This book sets out to 'tell them'.

The subtitle of this book is 'why there are no locks on the bathroom doors in the Hotel Louis XIV'. The Hotel (it has since burned down) was a modest one in Quebec. Each pair of bedrooms had a bathroom between then, reached by a door from each bedroom. Inside the bathroom, the user fixed a strap to the door handles at each end, so preventing the occupant of the other room from using the bathroom (the doors opened outwards). Equally, the user had to detach the strap to leave the bathroom, so there was no chance of locking the bathroom shut. This was a splendidly ingenious solution, except for the problems the strap creates in dividing the bathroom itself down the middle. Caplan enjoys pointing out the total absurdity of this solution. 'It was memorable as the total integration of object and circumstance', he called it, before going on to point out that most bathroom design is poor to inadequate, and so follows 'the tendency for inadequate designs to spawn product lines to make up for their inadequacy'. His technique is persuasion rather than castigation, for his object is to prove to his readers not just that design is possible or desirable but that it is necessary and feasible.

To this end he uses simple and evident examples to show that design is not an abstract quality but deeply interwoven into our everyday lives, and that, whether we are professionally involved with design or not, we are endlessly involved in design situations, and making decisions in which design plays a role. 'Chairs support more than bodies, they support body language', for example; 'teaching machines are unimaginative, but so were most of your teachers, remember?', or 'some gifts are for buying, selling and giving and have no other use'. With insight and wit he shows that design is a process in which all can be involved, and indeed are involved if only as consumers, and so understanding where design is coming from, and what its limitations are, is a duty we all owe ourselves. Caplan discusses the designer client relationship in some detail (as he says 'getting into bed with specialists carries the risk of exposure',) and concludes with an account of the work of Charles and Ray Eames (with whom he worked for many years).

Caplan's short book reads like an engaging fireside chat, full of memorable images (I particularly liked the tale of the New York school where, rather than trying the Sisyphean task of cleaning up graffiti, the janitor was given a magic marker and told to alter FUCK to BOOK whenever possible). But Caplan's plea is more subtle and important than that. It uses the particularly American technique of the simple narrator to demystify its subject and make it accessible, while making a strong case for the necessity of an informed dialogue on design – especially out there among the street signs.

News from the Front

ROBERT & JANET BLAICH
PRODUCT DESIGN & CORPORATE STRATEGY
McGraw Hill, New York, 1993

Shortly after the American designer Robert Blaich was appointed head of design at Philips, the giant Dutch electronics group in 1980, he made a presentation to the board about his plans for design in the company. At the end one of the director's leaned forward and asked sharply 'what is all this going to cost?' Blaich did not hesitate: 'Have you considered what the cost of having no design at all might be' he replied. What is surprising about the question is indeed its naiveté; Philips had been producing consumer electronic or electrical products for ninety years, so why hadn't they got behind the idea of design?

In part, as Blaich explains in his book *Product Design and Corporate Strategy*, written in 1992 after he left Philips, the reasons were historical. Philips had started in the Netherlands, a relatively small market, and had grown into a multinational through establishing national organizations in other countries round the world with responsibilities for marketing and also sometimes manufacturing, and a series of product divisions, not all located in Eindhoven, responsible for product development. Blaich calls the result a maze not a matrix – the private joke in the Philips Design Centre was that it was a pity there hadn't been a third Philips brother (the company was started in 1891 by two brothers, one an engineer and the other a salesman – if the third brother had been a designer...). The turf wars between national units created inefficiencies that were supplemented by duplicated manufacturing resources: it was clear to Blaich, and to several board members, including Dekker, the president-elect At the time, that major change was going to be needed to turn Philips from a staid multinational into a competitive global company, particularly in the light of competition, both in manufacturing and design, from Japan and South East Asia. Design, Blaich realized, could both be part of this change and act as an agent of change.

Even the Philips corporate identity was not as secure as it should be, Blaich realized. (The Philips name was too common to be copyrighted on its own, and so had to be turned into a mark that could be, for example). And a proper identity program would bring the national groups into line with the centre. So one of his first tasks was to create an identity manual, which was to be based on using Univers as a standard typeface and 100% cyan blue as a corporate colour: no printer or designer around the world could have difficulties with that. Shortly after the two volumes of he manual were produced and distributed, Blaich had a call from the head of marketing at one of the biggest national groups. The caller congratulated him on the new identity manual, which was long overdue, a Herculean task splendidly accomplished, very necessary, excellent example of

Roller 1 Radio, 1986

co-ordination and structured thinking: 'but', the caller con-
cluded, 'here we don't like Univers very much, so I think
we'll stick with Helvetica, if that's all right with you'.

Blaich realized that change had to be structural, working
across the whole organization, and not just delivered from
the top down, if it was to be effective. This meant that
product design had to be a managed process set firmly
within he main organizational structure. This involved for-
mulating design policies at a corporate level, maintaining
and improving professional standards, and harmonizing
products, systems, packaging and graphics to create a uni-
fied 'design face' for Philips. To achieve these the latest
skills and technologies had to be available. Most importantly, design had to be involved in the product creation
process from the start, not at the end. This involved not
only building teams for innovation on which designers were
represented equally with engineers and marketing experts,
but creating a team mentality in which such an approach
was acceptable. The achievement of this during Blaich's
tenancy was a major achievement and has been a major
factor in maintaining Philip's competitiveness since then.

Blaich's book, written jointly with his wife Janet, is not
just an account of his success at Philips (success documented also in John Heskett's 1989 book *Philips, A Study in
Design Management*). Blaich also draws on his earlier experience as a manager at Herman Miller, the American
furniture manufacturer for whim Charles Eames was for
many years design consultant, to frame both an argument
for the importance of design in product creation, and more
importantly, for the central role of design management in
good corporate practice. Its value lies in the fact that it
presents design management not just as theory, but in practice, and in two very different contexts. At Herman Miller,
the long association with the Eames and the work of George
Nelson had created an active design culture, fostered by top
management, but even so, as Blaich makes clear, the design
process needs to be managed and handled correctly.

Trained as an architect, Blaich joined Herman Miller in 1953 as a salesman, but moved rapidly into product management, working on the Eames Contract Storage System (a furniture system devised in the mid-1960s for university dormitories that fell victim to student unrest in the late 1960s, when college dormitories were abandoned in favour of living off campus), the Tandem Seating for O'Hare Airport, since used by countless other airports, and the Action Office Two System, a crash project for which he was head of design. Blaich's accounts of these projects, and of similar projects at Philips, take design out of the studio and into the hostile marketing meeting, the confrontation with competitors, and the risk-taking decision to launch into a new market. His particular experiences, related with enthusiasm, but also with an eye to the serious issues of corporate management and success (or failure) that they illustrate, provide a major contribution to the debate on design management.

Design management was a business buzz-word in the 1980s and early 1990s, even if a concept more often tokenly than actually supported in business. Certainly the mean and lean corporations that emerged, willingly or not, from the economic crises of the end of the 1980s, had learnt how to cost and invest prudently and strategically (a process often linked with a preference for getting out of manufacturing and into services, as a risk-avoidance strategy). But still today many companies, whose market success depends on their products and, particularly, their packaging, devolve design to too low a level and fail to maintain a proper design and identity strategy. As on packaging designer told me, when I asked what the design span of typical supermarket food product packages was, 'until the next marketing manager arrives!' Blaich's book deserves to be read by managers at all levels to understand the weakness of such a system. The cost of no design might be greater than you think.

Authoritative Thinking

CHRISTOPHER LORENZ
THE DESIGN DIMENSION
Blackwell, Oxford, 1987

The management editor of the Financial Times here attempts a marriage of two minds – to tell businessmen why
they need design, and in so doing explain to designers what
businessmen want from them. The argument is based on
case studies of a variety of businesses, including major
design-aware companies such as Olivetti and Sony, and re-
told classics such as John Deere tractors; the aim is to promote
design to equal status with marketing and technology in the
organisation of any manufacturing industry. In putting a
business premium on the primacy of design the author does
a considerable service to the serious appreciation of design.

The second edition also bravely insisted on the value of
original design and innovation, at a time when many
recession-hit manufacturers were reaching for the revamp
and the facelift. Tom Peters contributed his introduction
or perhaps his imprimatur, and the case studies were revised and extended, particularly the section on the development of the 'jelly-bean' Ford in the USA and Europe.
The success of the aerodynamic shape is taken as the success of design over Detroit: but jelly beans are crisp outside and sticky inside – was it the medium or the message
that really won? But such hesitations should not detract
from the direct arguments of this book. In particular,
Lorenz's analysis of the methods used by Japanese companies to infiltrate and in some cases dominate Western markets is particularly instructive. He draws attention to the
long-term nature of their management strategy, their market analysis and their development of designs based on research. This overall approach, in which design played an
integral part, enabled them to enter and finally control for

example the UK motorcycle business, and to make ground in the USA for small cars, despite such initial disasters as the Toypet.

While Olivetti and Sony can be seen as established examples of companies where there was a top-down, ingrained design culture, the same was not true of Philips, traditionally dominated by engineers, and in giving space to such a major European example Lorenz strengthens and boosts an argument that, at the time of publication, was almost heresy ('the corporation must not only undergo a radical shake-up in organisation, but a complete cultural revolution'). Bringing designers in at the beginning of the product development process was contrary to normal practice, which suggested you asked them to cheer the finished product up at the end. Lorenz describes this marketing rather than product-led syndrome as 'persistent myopia', among companies who had precious little idea of what marketing was about as a serious discipline anyway. Another of his case studies is of Baker Perkins, manufacturers of printing equipment – precisely the kind of technical area in which design, it might be thought, had little to offer. But he shows how Michael Baker, the CEO of Baker Perkins, 'converted' to industrial design and created world-beating products as a result.

Much of what Lorenz said then is today generally accepted: the necessity of continuous flexibility, the acceptance of change, the close definition of goals, even the importance of design. But his warnings about short term horizons and lack of persistence, about the failure to make design an equal partner with marketing (properly understood and applied) and technology, are as valid now as they were when he first wrote. Lorenz' status as a senior writer on the *Financial Times*, and his honed writing skills, made his book a salutary and important one. His untimely and early death meant that he did not have the possibility to develop his ideas further.

Styling the Suits

WALLY OLINS
CORPORATE IDENTITY
Thames & Hudson,   London 1989

Remember when Apple didn't mean computing, but music:
it was the label created by the Beatles in the late 1960s
to record themselves and their friends. This was the naïve
period of BritPop, as the music business is now called. We
cheerfully assumed, as we paid 8/5d each Saturday for the
new 45 rpm single, that the nexus between money and
music hardly existed: what did the Fab Four want their
own label for?

We are a bit wiser today: while the Beatles seemed to have
a musical and social logic behind their success, the Spice
Girls existed only as a marketable proposition, not a musical one. The music business has emerged from Tin Pan
Alley into Wall Street, into a visibly mediated, designed,
and commercial enterprise.

The original Apple record logo was designed, thirty years ago, by the new design firm of Wolff Olins, a young Englishman and a young Dane who had teamed up to provide design services not just in graphics but in the newly emerging field of corporate identity. Wolff Olins have lasted rather longer than the Apple logo they designed, a fact celebrated in Wally Olins' *Corporate Identity*, published in 1989 (Wolff had left some time before to pursue other interests). At that time Wolff Olins was among the top design agencies in the UK specialising in corporate identity, called in to consult for government agencies, for multinationals and large British companies, and for design-aware and ambitious brands.

What Wally Olins had realised was that in the term 'corporate identity design' the first two words were as important as the third. Put another way, design elegance was by no means the whole solution to the brief. The design had in some way to embody the personality of the corporation, so making it recognisable (not just memorable) both within the corporation, and to outsiders at different levels (customers, bankers, shareholders and so forth). Thus the test of a new identity, in Olins' view, was

not the design quality of the final graphic solution, important as this was, but the way in which it provided a means for the company to be recognised, and the way it defined how the company did what it did. More than just a mirror, it could also be an agent of change, often as much within the company as towards the company's external partners.

Olins seeks to set out the validity of this approach, to root it in a historical perspective reaching back to battle flags and mediaeval coats of arms, and to relate the concept of identity to the concept of branding (a phenomenon that developed in the late nineteenth century). He is also concerned to show how a managed system for corporate identity can enhance a company's competence and performance. To demonstrate the process, he invents an American conglomerate, the Buffalo & Santa Fe Railroad, which has since the heady days of steam moved into all kinds of disparate markets, and tries to show how a designer would tackle a brief to make some sense of it all. Probably because of its invented nature, this account rings rather

Preceding pages: identity for the Portuguese Tourist Board, and leaflets for Boehringer Ingelheim, by Wolff Olins

hollow (and produces some terrible puns, such as the Buff & Shine bootpolish concept) though it does demonstrate the issues.

The arguments that Olins puts forward, and the methods he describes, could still be heard in any design consultancy working with identity and branding today. The language has become more technical, and the broad-brush issues Olins discusses are now broken down into more detailed elements: in particular the disciplines of branding and identity have developed almost independent status. But Olins was one of a group of British-based design consultants who moved design onto the corporate centre stage during the 1980s, For example, one major project that Wolff Olins undertook in the early 1990s was to reorganise and give a structure to the different groups of hotels owned by Trust House Forte. It was a complex issue and Wolff Olins solution gave the group much clearer visibility in a crowded marketplace. And when a few years later the group was the target of a hostile take-over bid, one of the first experts they called in to help defend them was Wally Olins.

Facing and above: promotional material for Orange telecommunications by Wolff Olins

Toys for the Boys

STEPHEN BAYLEY
SEX, DRINK AND FAST CARS
Faber & Faber, London, 1987

Stephen Bayley is one of a generation of writers who applied the lessons of the New Journalism with vigour and
wit to the brave new world of design. Also, as curator of
the Boilerhouse Gallery in the Victoria & Albert Museum
and then as first director of the Conran-funded Design
Museum in the Docklands, he had an important influence
on how design was presented to the British public. Exhibitions such as Coke and National Characteristics in Design
set an agenda for presenting design as culture and communication as much as form and function.

Sex, Drink and Fast Cars is a cheerful history of our contemporary fascination with automobiles. It covers some of
the same ground as Bayley's first book, a study of Harley
Earl, the chief designer at General Motors in the post-war
period. In that book Bayley looked at how Earl's exuber-
ant sense of design reflected (in chrome) the social aspirations and cultural values of middle-class America, quite
unconcerned with any notion of functionality or sense of
efficiency. An elegant proof that modernism could not be
used to explain the design history of the American car:
what Earl had was a wholly populist imagination operating in a demand-led market. The fact that the resulting
products were robust in no validation of their design, rather another facet of the material abundance that made it
possible to create them.

The title of *Sex, Drink and Fast Cars* comes from a com-
miserating conversation with a friend who had just passed
his fortieth birthday: 'yes', replied the friend, 'from now

on its just sex, drink and fast cars'. Given this toys for boys agenda, it is not surprising that Bayley devotes quite some time to motor racing, elegantly exploring the paradoxes between motion and danger, speed and safety that are at the heart of Formula One. The story of the death of James Dean acts as a coda to this, and Bayley also evokes the roles of cars as characters in literature and film, from the anodyne pastel of Herbie to the horror mobile of Stephen King's Clarrie. The writing is literate, informed and often witty, the arguments subtle. The relevance of this book lies in the quality of the writing: it persuaded mainstream publishers that design could be offered to the non-specialist and sold successfully. Faber, who publish this book, were known for their fiction and poetry lists and for some serious scholarship on fine and applied art. But not for design. A similar but less subtle book was Deyan Sudjic's *Cult Objects,* published by Paladin (part of Harper Collins) for whom illustrated paperback books were a rarity. This too sought to offer the general public a quick tour of contemporary design and designers – mainly through product design and fashion.

Books that aim to define the zeitgeist tend to have a hard time of it: too much effort goes into appearing not to be trying too hard. The real successes are the unexpected ones – *Zen and the Art of Motorcycle Maintenance* or *A Brief History of Time* are in their very different ways books which unconsciously speak to and so define the needs and desires of a particular moment in time. To do justice to what has been termed 'the twentieth century's love affair with the automobile' requires more than one book and one approach: but what Bayley does achieve is to give a design dimension to the tale.

Aftermaths and Forwards

PETER DORMER
DESIGN SINCE 1945
Thames & Hudson, London, 1993

The Second World War marks a hiatus in design history: firms manufacturing consumer goods turned to war work, 'commercial artists', as graphic designers were called at the time, were drafted into the forces, or in some cases into work for the propaganda ministries. There were some attempts during the war to set design standards (the Utility programme in Britain is one example). With the end of the war, getting industry back into peacetime mode in the Allied countries and putting industries back together in Germany, Italy and Japan became the pressing problems, something reflected in the fact that the emblem of the *Wirtschaftswunder*, as German economic recovery was called, was the Volkswagen Beetle, a pre-war design that had never been manufactured in quantity before. The end of the war also made available technological developments for commercial exploitation, and the demographic changes brought about by the war, particularly in the USA, created new markets for consumer goods.

It can therefore be argued that post-war conditions were sufficiently different from pre-war to allow treating the history of design as falling into two parts. It is certainly true that the rate of change in technology, particularly print and communications media such as television, became much faster after the war, and that the trend towards global products became more marked, partly because of the American hegemony in the aftermath of the war, and again once the Japanese began in the 1970s to penetrate world markets. It can also be argued that post-war optimism about the potential of design, shown through the Good

Design exhibitions organised at the Museum of Modern Art in New York and the work of the Design Council in Britain, shows that design was seen as a social and economic force in new ways, and presaged the greater role design was going to play both in government and industry. Design has become part of a cultural mix, together with fashion and music, in which the accessories in the home are lined up with the clothes in the wardrobe as tools to enable individuals to express and define themselves. If in the 1930s it was clothing that marked out different groups in society, today, it could be argued, the distinctions are drawn as well on the type of Walkman or wristwatch you have.

This is not the story of design that Peter Dormer chooses to tell. His fine book should perhaps have been entitled 'designers since 1945', since an important part of his focus is on the nature and role of the design profession. From this perspective the important distinction between the post- and pre-war periods is the emergence of the design team, and the integration of the design function into corporate structures. It is certainly true that the designers who created the profession of industrial designer in the USA before the war, like Teague, Loewy and Bel Geddes, worked as independents, being hired *ad hoc* to solve particular problems, and that after the war companies like General Motors and IBM moved rapidly to an integrated design structure, even if these systems were dominated by individual personalities such as Harley Earl and George Nelson.

Dormer therefore draws on the story of companies such as Philips and Olivetti to show design taking this new role, which, as he shows, was linked to a vision of design as a rational and practical activity, almost a science. In this context the work of Scandinavian designers on natural form, and researches into ergonomics and industrial efficiency, play an important part. By focussing in the first half of the book on industrial and product design, he is able to present very cogently his argument that the designer is a member of a team. 'Design', he writes, 'subservient to manufacturing, the market and the consumer, is seen as an evolutionary process rather than a series of inspirations. This is not to deny the role of the individual as a driving force in design, but it is to dilute the importance of "self-expression"'. After the hyping of design in the 1980s, this is a useful correlative.

Unfortunately, the slightly formulaic arrangement of the book blunts this argument somewhat. After three opening chapters on 'What is a Designer?' 'Industrial and Product Design', and 'The Style of Product Design', he turns to looking at different design fields: graphics, furniture, domestic ware and textiles, with a concluding chapter on design futures. While these topic chapters are full of useful information, the format imposed by the publishers does not allow any of these subjects to be dealt with adequately: furniture design alone would fill the available space, while the chapter on textile design also tries to touch on fashion.

In the closing chapter Dormer returns to his original theme, pointing out that it is in the nature of late twentieth century design to be involved not only with the appearance and formal values of objects but their social significance as well. This is desirable in itself: design should be seen as a system for solving problems not as decoration. But this also draws the designer deeper into the team, involving him or her with other aspects of the client's business than the immediate brief, and inviting design work to relate top society at large. Dormer's thesis is a useful correlative to some hero-based accounts of design, and deserves a wide audience.

The Italian Job

VARIOUS EDITORS
INTERNATIONAL DESIGN YEARBOOK
Calmann & King, London 1983 to date

Paris in the springtime, perhaps, but definitely Milan in April, if you have any interest in furniture design. For that's the season for the Salone del Mobile, a week of gossip and discovery, staged events and unexpected trouvailles. For Milan, unlike any other trade fair I know of, has both an on-site and and off-site element: the nearest comparison is the mainstream Edinburgh Festival and the Edinburgh Fringe. The distinction is important in Milan, for while the official fiera takes place over ten or so pavillions in the main municiapl fairgrounds, much of the material shown in the official event can only politely be described as humdrum. Reproducton Garibaldi commodes (or whatever the Italian equivalent of Seconde Empire is), garden furniture in polypropylene disguised as marble, fake rusticity for fake rustics (read city-dwellers in their second homes) occupy eighty percent of the official space. Only a couple of areas are given over to contemporary design. It is salutary to bear this disproportion in mind when one considers that Italy has a global reputation for contemporary furniture design, with the Milan Salone as its supposed epicentre.

But the off-site, 'Fringe' space is, for those seriously interested in furniture design, the real fair. The mainstream manufacturers show concept products, the non-Italian outsiders find a more congenial locations for their experiments. This diaspora has created its own highlights: the joint show of new wonders by the German lighting designer Ingo Maurer and the Anglo-Israelian sculptor Ron Arad is one, the unveiling of new probings of form and material by the Dutch co-operative group Droog Design is another. Italian designers have also used off-site for special occasions, the most famous of which is the launch of the Memphis Collection by Sottsass, de Lucchi and others in 1981, a truly if unruly ground-breaking event in furniture design.

Shortly after the launch of Memphis the design consultant Stuart Durant suggested to the publishers Calmann & King that a design annual featuring each year's new furniture, textile, lighting, houseware and product design would be a good idea. From this the International Dersign Yearbook was born. Each year a call for entries goes out to designers worldwide in the related fields, supported by intensive research that includes a team visit to Milan to gather up the novelties of the year. The results are then judged by an invited designer, commented and captioned, organised and published.   The designers invited to make the selection include Philippe Starck, Robert Stern, Emilio Ambasz, Alessandro Mendini, Andree Putnam, Jean Nouvel, Jasper Morrison and Ron Arad. At the time of writing the millenial selection – for the year 2000 edition – is being made by Ingo Maurer.

Here I must admit to a personal involvement: for three years I was lucky enough to be invited by the publishers to act as general editor, working with the guest designer making the selection to organise and arrange the choice. This involved selecting 400 items from some 3,000 entries. While from the personality and tastes of the selector it was always possible to guess some of the work that would be selected in advance, there were always unexpected choices which when seen with the whole made sense. Thus the book could be read in two ways: as a cross-section of recent and interesting work in the different fields, or as the taste of the particular selector. In the first few years after it began, the *Design Yearbook* was one of the best authoritative sources for new design. But as the lifestyle magazines began to find design, especially for furniture and housewares, worth publishing in some detail, so the book as a source of new information (except in product design, a subject that seems to terrify other publishers) became less important, while the personality of the selector, and the arguments advanced for his or her selection, became more important. And across the run of annual volumes it became possible to follow the development of the work of individual designers.

The strength of the *International Design Yearbook* is its continuity, its regularity of offer, and its production values. Its weakness lies also, ironically, in its regularity, which can lead to an assumption that it can be pushed in the wrong direction (emphasising the graphic design of the medium rahter than the work is is supposed to showcase, for example, or selecting a design solution that fails to match the quality of the choice or express the issues that the selector wishes to raise). But it has, as a series, been a witness of design's growing role and importance, and of the increasing sophistication of the issues around contemporary three-dimensional design.

Graphics are Great

Hands-on History

SEBASTIAN CARTER
TWENTIETH CENTURY TYPE DESIGNERS
Trefoil, London, 1987

'Speaking of earlier types, Goudy says: 'The old fellows steal all of our best ideas'. Sebastian Carter uses this quotation from the American type designer Frederic W. Goudy as an example of his Italian Old Face of 1924, but it could in some ways stand as an epigraph for a great deal of type design. It has elegance, wit and a grudging respect for the past. (I liked the quote so much that at one time I printed it up on a postcard, only to realise afterwards that outside a typographic context it did not make quite as much sense).

The story of typeface design in the early part of the twentieth century is dominated, in Britain at least, by the figure of Stanley Morison, who in 1929 first began advising *The Times* about modernising their typefaces. The resulting design, Times New Roman, is probably still the most widely used Western typeface in the world. Morison went on to encourage others to redesign their existing faces, often going back to the original Renaissance models from which they had strayed over the centuries. In doing this he restored a good deal of dignity to traditional sansserif typefaces, and encouraged other designers either in creating faces based on old models, or in designing new ones.

The work of Eric Gill and Berthold Wolpe in Britain, and of Jan Tschichold in Switzerland (and later in Britain), William Addison Dwiggins and Goudy in the USA, and Rudolph Kock in Germany benefited from Morison's example, though each has a quality and tradition of its own. This group designed mainly for metal typefaces, but the development of lithographic printing from films, not from metal type, created new opportunities for a second generation of designers, notably Adrien Frutiger and Hermann Zapf. Designing for film (and later for digitized) type sets different challenges, while appearing to free up the designer from the physical restraints of metal. With the conversion to film-based systems in the 1970s, the history of type design reached a natural turning point, though not all conversions of metal types to film were happy ones. And since this book was first published, the development of digital printing and the rise of desk-top publishing systems and subsequently the arrival of the World Wide Web, has changed the rules of the game completely.

The idea of a book of essays on the main type designers and their contribution was first suggested by the poet and printer, Asa Benveniste, but he felt the task would make too many claims on his time, and we therefore approached Sebastian Carter, a calligrapher and designer/printer. He brought to the book not merely an extensive knowledge of the history of type, but – perhaps more importantly – a working knowledge of type, which echoes through his comments on the types and their creators. One of the most difficult decisions was in which type to set the book (which Carter himself designed). He finally selected Ehrhardt, a type designed by Morison on the basis of a Frankfurt type from 1710, itself modelled on an earlier Hungarian face.

The history of type design, in particular in the rediscoveries and new technologies it has undergone in the twentieth century, is a reminder that communication through type is still a key activity for designers. Despite whatever the current cries may be heard about the end of print and the death of the book (cries that are often issued in printed form) the ability to handle type well will continue to be a major design skill. If those behind the twentieth-century renaissance in type design might now be seen as conservative in their attitudes, they at least created a wealth of options for their successors to explore and exploit.

Ordering the Letters

HERMANN ZAPF
ABOUT ALPHABETS
MIT Press, Boston, 1980

The only effing problem type designers have is apparently just that: the letter f is one of the most difficult to
design and co-ordinate within a typeface, especially in a
serif typeface such as this book is set in. That's according to Hermann Zapf, author of *About Alphabets*, and one
of the most prolific and internationally successful type designers of post-war Europe.

This small and compact book has a complex history: the
text was originally commissioned by the Typophiles club
in New York and issued as a chapbook in 1970: a decade
later MIT Press reissued it in the present format, with a
series of extended interpolated commentaries extending the
original text. These are set close-spaced to distinguish them
from the wider spaced original, and this extended text is
complemented by a series of illustrations (printed on text
paper) of various Zapf-designed faces and ornaments, and
a number of preliminary sketches and developmental drawings for these. The appearance of the whole is of an elegant homage between fellow professionals expanded for a
wider but still coherent readership. By coherent, I mean a
readership that accepted classical typeface design as the
benchmark, that was adjusting to photocomposed faces but
with a nostalgic feeling for hot metal and hand-composed
type, and who, if they were aware of the revolution in
type processing waiting to happen through personal computers and desktop publishing programs, did not understand it at all. For the computer revolution changed fun-
damentally the parameters within which type composition
(and so type design) operated.

Zapf's original text, on a straight reading, is a modest biography, explaining what drew him into type design, and which types he designed and when, and how the influences and demands that shaped their individual design arose. The opening illustration of the MIT edition is of a calligraphed quotation from Cobden-Sanderson concerning the imperative for a type designer never to come between the reader and the author, and Zapf's account of his work and life seems to share the same reticence: the quiet craftsman working with care and love.

A closer reading of the original text and the later additions suggests, however, that what we have here is rather different. The additions, in particular, carry a note of confidence that illuminates some parts of the original in a revealing way. By confidence I am not suggesting an affluence of arrogance on Zapf's part (not that he shouldn't be entitled to a certain pride in his achievement). Rather the distance between Zapf and his original readers becomes that much clearer, and its significance with it.

The story of type design in Britain, and to a certain extent in the USA, in the first half of the twentieth century, is the account of re-establishing proper standards in type after the indulgent and laissez-faire attitudes of the Victorian era. And the criterion for those standards was the past: the classic faces created by Italian printers in the Renaissance or French typecutters in the Siécle de la Lumière. This process, for example in the hands of Stanley Morison, was in large part a honest process of good husbandry, taking typefaces that had evolved randomly, through ignorance rather than design, back to a clear original and redefining them. But is was also a historicist process: its underlying assumption was that traditional typefaces could contain all that could be desired. Or as the great American designer Frederick Goudy memorably summed up the problem facing contemporary designers 'the old fellows stole all our best ideas'.

While Zapf's text follows the precepts of personal modesty and respect for the past expected of type designers' memoirs (a mode set in part by the writings of Simon and Morison) he in fact has nothing to do with such a tradition, and wants nothing to do with it either. He is not codifying past types for present consumption (a role Morison appointed himself to) rather he is creating new types for a new Germany in a new world, for which the past was a reference but not a binding example.

There is often in English thinking an assumption that knowledge of the past binds you to an acceptance of its values and their continuing relevance (only in England could a political party called 'Conservative' be considered a serious force). Zapf is perfectly well aware that the problems he is facing in designing new types (both for metal setting and photocomposition) have occupied others in the past, who in turn found elegant solutions to them. He too looks at classical models for inspiration (Trajan's Column in Rome and stonework inscriptions in the Santa Croce cemetery in Florence, at one point). But his mastery of historic type designs does not make him their slave.

Rather he is designing new faces for a new world. This is in part, as he points out with due modesty, to meet a market need. After the end of the Second World War traditional black-letter or fraktur types were largely abandoned in Germany, partly to draw a line over the past, partly to move into a more modern mode, for the varied demands of modern printing presses, printing surfaces and media. So there was a demand for new roman letterforms. Zapf believed in progress, and of the role of print in progress. And, as he says 'progress demands courage; and as the powers of conservatism were and are always in the majority, they will not stop the entire development, they can only retard it'.

Reading the Signs

PETER WILDBUR & MICHAEL BURKE
INFORMATION GRAPHICS
Thames & Hudson, London, 1999

An expert in the design and management of conference centres once pointed out to me the basic fallacy behind any signage system: 'they fail', he said, 'to cater for those users who don't look where they are going until they are lost!' Stories of drivers spending hours on urban orbital motorway systems such as London's M25 in the happy belief that they are on their way to Scotland support this view: signs only work if they are seen, and also understood.

Peter Wildbur is a skilled navigator in the world of signage: his first book on information graphics appeared the 1960s, before even Tufte's classic *The Visual Display of Quantative Information*, which is also one of the great self-publishing success stories of all time. His most recent book is co-authored by Michael Burke, who is professor of graphics at Schwabisch Gmund in Germany. They approach their subject – innovative solutions in contemporary design – not through a typology of information systems but by grouping solutions according to purpose. Chapters are headed 'Informing the Traveller', 'Explaining how Things Work', 'Controlling the Input', and so on. In each chapter, alongside a general discussion and pages of examples of solutions, there is at least one long case study of a specific project written by one of the designers responsible, and explaining the background to the project and the design process. Since the main intended audience for the book seems to be design students and young designers, this has the excellent effect of giving the feel of real projects, as well as setting out 'best practice' examples in information graphic design.

The examples they show have been gathered from around the world, and include not only conventional signage but on-screen and multimedia systems as well. Among the most elegant of the examples they cite are the semicircular displays used on one scenic route by Swiss Railways to enable travellers to identify the various landmarks they pass. Here the authors note that the development of multimedia has been driven, not unexpectedly, by software engineers rather than designers. (The same problems occurred in the development of early photosetting systems: in the breakthrough of getting letters onto film from a computer, the letterform detail got lost). They therefore argue strongly for the involvement of designers at the start of the development process, especially for new technologies. The analysis they offer of the information problems related to solid user interfaces (integrated independent systems to control individual machines) is particularly pertinent, and they manage to avoid the cliché of adults unable to programme VCR machines.

Information signs at the Domaine de Chambord, France

Despite the excellent introductions to each section, the case studies, and the use of multiple illustrations with full captions for other projects (often given a whole page or a spread) there is a slight sense of frustration in reading this book. This I think stems in part from a Cartesian curiosity about the individual projects: one wants to know more about how they work. It also comes from the way we look at things, particularly in the case of information on screen (which it is, as the authors point out, very difficult to show in the case of interactive media, however much space is available). Traditionally information graphics either followed the heirarchies of print: left to right, top to bottom, or used pictograms or abstract forms to convey single items of information. The invention of cinema and radio, and early television, replaced this structure with a similar sequential order based on time. But new media do not follow or need to follow such organisations and levels of information (indeed some research indicates that teenagers today make a kind of visual 'screen grab' of whole groups of data and then analyse them in detail at random).

It could be argued indeed that the invention of the on-screen icon controlled by the mouse on the Apple Mac represents both a melding of these two forms of information and carried them together into a new dimension. This goes beyond clicking a button to continue, rather than turning a page. The apparatus of toolbars, pull-down menus and embedded links found not just in web-based documents but almost any document consulted on screen requires a different kind of 'reading' for the user to gain full benefit from it, and allows the user paths through a document which are not wholly determined by the author. The authors are emphatic that these new modes of vision will demand more subtlety from information designers in the future, but what those subtleties will be, the authors leave as an open question: apart from, quite rightly, asserting that we will need better design as the pace of the information revolution increases.

Macintosh Woman

LIZ FARRELLY
**APRIL GREIMAN :
FLOATING IDEAS IN TIME AND SPACE**
Thames & Hudson, London, 1999

The Swiss publisher Lars Muller once expressed very simply the value of understanding history in contemporary
design. 'Of course students look at the work of David Carson and April Greiman and take it as a starting point. Our
job is to remind them that Carson and Greiman had their
starting points too'. In Greiman's case this was the Basel
Design School in Switzerland. She had chosen Basel
because of the city's connections with Jung, whose writing on myths, symbols and the psyche she had discovered
while studying at Kansas. But by a happy chance at Basel
she was taught, among others, by Wolfgang Weingart, head
of typography. He was busy breaking every rule he could
find in the quest for typographical expressionism, and Greiman was to develop her own style through his approach
and her understanding of Jung.

After graduate study at Basel, and working for Emilio Ambasz at the Museum of Modern Art in New York, she
moved 'accidentally', as she puts it, to California. Here the
discovery of the desert landscape and the arrival in the
design world of the Apple Macintosh were to unleash her
potential. Working with a small team of colleagues in an
environment that was as much a research centre as a design agency, Grieman was to find a range of clients, often from design schools and museums, notably the Southern California Institute of Architecture (SCI-Arc), as well
as corporate clients such as Vitra, who saw her talents as
appropriate for the contemporary, often multi-cultural vi-

sion they wished to express. Her use of colour, layering and sizing of type created a metaphorical vocabulary of considerable complexity. This moved on from expression only in printed media to website design, identities for restaurants, interiors, environments and exhibitions. Grieman herself describes her clients as 'coming to me wanting advice on what they should do' rather than with a written brief. And seeing herself not just as providing a design service, in her own writing, notably her 1990 book *Hybrid Imagery: the Fusion of Technology and Graphic Design*, she describes the design process used in her work in detail, both in terms of the use of technology and the conceptual framework that shapes it.

Grieman is an articulate and committed designer, whose work has a content that goes beyond its initial remit into social and political commentary, and seeks to establish a set of true values for its users. 'A sheet of paper isn't merely a neutral receiver of symbols, but a field of space that is traversed', she comments, summing up the central concept of the New Typography, which is that the hierarchies of order that applied in the analogue era have no place in the digital age. In this respect she and the other 'new typographers' such as Brody and Carson, can be seen as the exemplars of the vision of the future set out by Marshall McLuhan, as well as being creative people with their own philosophies and agendas. But for all the skill of Liz Farrelly's writing, the scope of this book is too small and its approach too formulaic to allow enough of the depth of Grieman's achievement to show through.

Cyberspaces & Multi-Realities

VirtualVision head-up VR display, 1994

Cyberspace Discovered

WILLIAM GIBSON
NEUROMANCER / COUNT ZERO / MONA LISA OVERDRIVE
Ace Publishing, New York, 1984-6

'This is a Rolls Royce', Sebastian explained, 'they built a good car, in the old days, the Arabs'. Many science fiction writers have tried to portray the confusions and false histories of a future world after a massive disaster: most of them concentrate on the physical destruction, genetic mutations or reversals of political power an event such as a nuclear exchange might provoke. Gibson takes the post-apocalypse landscape but leaves its origins – whether in war or industrial pollution or both – unclear, preferring to explore the social and cultural effects of global change. The first result of this approach is a text of radical density, bristling with meanings and dark wit – the punishment for grand theft auto is induced Korsakov's syndrome, for example, while the Turing police supervise artificial intelligences.

Gibson's main innovation, however, is to take the idea of an information superhighway and meld it with the idea of virtual reality to create cyberspace. This is a fully-animated, three-dimensional virtual environment, called the matrix, in which databases, memory stores and computer information appear as visible, tangible structures. The matrix is a heaven for hackers – jockeys in the text – whose gateway to it is the neural plug – called a microsoft, inevitably but brilliantly nonetheless – that wires the brain directly into the virtual world. Much of the action of the books in the trilogy takes place on this interface between reality and virtuality. The rest of the action takes place in cities

which have become emblematized: Chiba as the best location for spare parts surgery, London as the celebration of
'gomi' (Japanese for rubbish) and New York (now part of
the Sprawl) as home of the cyberjockeys and a certain
residual media power. Not forgetting the Moon: a lunar
Las Vegas plus (remember Apollo) graveyard of the ambi-
tions of space exploration.

What is important about Gibson's trilogy is that it has
become, in bizarre fashion, some kind of a blueprint for
the design and development of computer technologies and
a framework for the discussion of new personal and cultural relations in a virtual society: this is like NASA turning to Stanley Kubrick (or Arhtur C. Clarke, on whose
story *2001* was based) for advice on the Shuttle missions.
It is a tribute to the force of Gibson's argument and the
quality of his writing, and an acknowledgement that the
cyberworld, if or when it comes about, will require both
imagination and technology, and that the metaphors for
describing and understanding it did not exist before. Gibson's premise that information is the hardest currency of
all has recently come true in the stock market flotation of
software companies such as Superscape, Pixar and Net-
scape, for example (adjust examples on weekly basis to
suit). And don't forget Gibson's own comment made in a
UK Channel 4 interview, a decade after his books were
published: 'the two things that have surprised me most in
recent history were the fall of Soviet Russia and the explosive growth of the Internet and World Wide Web'.

Blade Runner

PHILIP K DICK
DO ANDROIDS DREAM OF ELECTRIC SHEEP?
Doubleday, New York, 1968

Ask a designer to name a few favourite films, and *Blade-runner*, the Ridley Scott film based on Dick's novel, will probably be somewhere in the list. There are several possible reasons for this. One is the astonishing visual virtuosity of the film, which creates a stunning image of a post-apocalypse American city, colonising space but abandoning earth, using humanoid robots – the androids of the original title. Another reason, perhaps less charitable, is that in making the film Scott made a major career move, from directing extremely successful television commercials to making real movies, something any designer of calibre would die for. A third is the conceit of the androids themselves: wholly human, immensely powerful, yet remote and confused. The closing emotion in the film is a sense of loss that such astonishing machines should have failed, and knew that they failed.

The Bladerunners are a despised elite (the sort Dick prefers) who keep the earth free of androids. The plot of the film and the book starts with the Bladerunners being called in to find a group of androids who have escaped from an asteroid and are roaming earth. This simple thriller becomes complexified, partly by the nature of the androids themselves, and the angst of the hero, and by brilliant film technique, that creates a series of lasting and convincing surreal images of a polyglot market place, the first cyber-slum, which makes the Bladerunner's quest both futile and ironic. There is, however, a marked contrast between book and film. In the book the Bladerunner fails, and returns to an inadequate life, having seen and partly understood the android option, but failed to rise to it. In the film Harrison Ford sets off into the sunrise – into landscape out of cityscape – with the ambiguous prize of an android lover. Scott takes enormous liberties with the narrative of the book, but captures much of its essence. Given the generally flaccid 'film of the book' served up by the film industry, *Bladerunner* is an astonishing work for this achievement alone.

Much of Philip K. Dick's early writing was in the form of short stories sold to magazines. One magazine editor, not an early admirer of Dick, was converted on reading a story in which Dick convincingly presented the use of marmalade as currency: after that, he decreed, Dick could sell him anything he wanted. Dick's work is shot through with ambiguity, anomie and despair but carries, through the quality of his writing, an ineffable conviction. One of his best novels, *The Man in the High Castle,* posits a German/Japanese victory in World War Two, leading to a servile America striving to find an identity between the wholly opposite ideologies of the I'Ching and Nazism. Dick opts for the Taoist position, with a certain dark relish.

Science fiction can be seen as design without limits: anything is possible, but the concept must be coherent. That a visual designer such as Ridley Scott could take the complexities of *Do Androids Dream* and turn it into a new and equally powerful icon of its own is a confirmation of the necessity for designer to dream too.

Living the Wired Way

NICHOLAS NEGROPONTE
BEING DIGITAL
Simon & Schuster, New York, 1996

The first time Nicholas Negroponte saw the words of his
new book *Being Digital* on paper was when the publishers sent him a proof copy. As befits one of the leading
figures in the development of computer software and computing concepts, through his work at MIT, first in ArchMac
and now at the Media Lab, the whole book was written
on screen and delivered to the publisher on disc. Yet there
is an irony in this: why go back to the technology of
Gutenberg when the Internet is on the doorstep? Part of
the reason offered by Negroponte is that many of decision
makers, whether in industry, business, society and politics
have little understanding of what the information revolution is doing, and even fewer use the technology directly,
so that a book is a way of reaching this important but
out-of-touch group. Surprisingly, though he does mention
his regular (and very interesting) column in the American
edition of *Wired* magazine, the idea that books remain a
successful way of conveying data is not one of the reasons
he gives.

Certainly Negroponte does not make assumptions about
the prior knowledge of his readers. Its clear style and absence of jargon is one of the book's major strengths, in
that it presents the present state and potential value of the
revolution in computing, communications and the media
with ease and clarity. Negroponte's central argument is that
the information age is here already, and that we need to
change our ways of thinking and defining categories to ac-
commodate the fundamental changes that are already in
train. One of the key concepts he discusses is the differ-

ences between bits and atoms, between information (digital bits) and media (books, tapes, discs and so on). This is vital because today information is no longer dependent on its medium, but can, in digital form, be passed through any number of media. He tells the story of being asked by the security desk of a major computer chip manufacturer the value of the laptop computer he was carrying into a meeting. 'Between one and two million dollars', he replied, thinking of the importance of the information on the machine's hard disc. 'Oh no, sir', was the reply, 'a Powerbook cannot be worth more than $2,000', as the receptionist was thinking about the atoms not the bits.

Another important concept is that of the computer as agent rather than tool. this is an idea also set out some time ago by John Walker, the founder of Autodesk, and Negroponte extends his argument to the role of the personal computer as an entity that interacts with and 'knows' the user, able, like an electronic Jeeves, to analyse situations and offer suggestions as well as execute commands and routines. This also assumes the extension of the computer into wider and wider areas of business and domestic life (I particularly liked the idea of the smart toaster, able to link into the news and imprint the headlines onto the breakfast muffin...). Negroponte's advocacy of the nature and potential of the new technology is powerful and fair, and this book should be required reading for anyone interested in the role computers are going to play in society.

Alphanumerically Speaking

BOB COTTON & RICHARD OLIVER
THE CYBERSPACE LEXICON
Phaidon, London, 1994

The first letter I turned to in the Cyberspace Lexicon was G, to see what the book had to say about William Gibson, who invented the term in his novel Neuromancer. Gigabytes yes, Goraud shading, yes, Gibson, no. Gibson's name (and credit for his idea) is to be found under C for Cyberspace. Here at once is one of the main oddities of the cyberspace debate. This wholly fictional concept, sited in an undetermined future, is cited as an actual, independent notion, a blueprint for the real future. This is like using Ferriss's *Metropolis of Tomorrow* as a street plan of Manhattan. In this process of colonising cyberspace the wit, irony and darkness of Gibson's trilogy is thrown away as well. Cyberspace has ceased to be a visionary concept, and become a catch-phrase. So it is in this book.

That said, the authors offer a comprehensive, lucid and well-illustrated account of current developments in multimedia, virtual reality and computing. Malcolm Garrett's dynamic design, and a wide range of images, make the reader into a voyager into new technology. In visual/information terms, the book probably comes as close as anything on paper can to an interactive publication. From synthespians via the horizontal blanking period to blitter and yuv, anything you need to know about the information revolution is to be found here.

There main drawback of the book is at one with its slippery title. While strong on information and research content, even the longer descriptive texts adopt a passive pose. The relentless optimism of those already working in the field fills every page. They are, after all, entitled, as pioneers, to their enthusiasm, but more critical distance should be expected from the authors.

The social issues of access and privacy, and the philosophical issues of defining reality and perception in the new media (to take but two examples) are as important to us all as the nature of the new hardware. Significantly, neither Mitchell's *The Reconfigures Eye* (MIT Press, 1992) nor Woolley's *Virtual Worlds* appears in the bibliography, nor are the issues raise in those books addressed except in passing. Mitchell's redefinitions of perception, starting with the geometries of perspective and ending in the digital age, are essential for an understanding of the ways contemporary visual information is to be analysed. Mitchell has since explored the urban implications of the digital world in his *City of Bits* (MIT Press, 1995). Benjamin Woolley's analysis links scientific discoveries, particularly in the areas of nuclear physics and chaos theory, to an analysis of contemporary modes of vision, and to developments in information theory.

The Lexicon authors' definition of cyberspace, somewhat ungramatically, is 'the interconnected web of databases, telecommunications links and computer networks which perceptually seem to constitute a new space for human communications and actions'. William Gibson call cyberspace 'a graphic representation of data abstracted from the banks of every computer in the human system. Unaccountable complexity. Lines of light ranged in the nonspace of the mind, clusters and constellations of data. Like city lights, receding'. To understand hypermedia we need not just facts, but some visions too.

Keeping out of the Net

IAIN BOAL & JAMES BROOK (EDITORS)
RESISTING THE VIRTUAL LIFE
City Lights, San Francisco, 1995

The Luddites have had a bad press, historically. School books portrayed them as heavy-handed rustics destroying machines and their makers with the fervour and ignorance of cannibals boiling up missionaries (another Victorian myth). This simplistic version ignores the real claims of the Luddites, their selectivity in only destroying machines that destroyed communities, and the horrible fact that, thanks to a special Act of Parliament, many were hanged for their crimes. The Luddites argued for a structured use of machinery in industry, that would not create destitution for many in return for wealth for a few.

The current electronic information environment, newly personified by the Internet, should attract similar concerns and suspicions. This notion of the state and international business, both ruthlessly hungry for data on each and every one, as newly enabled by technology to probe even further into individual privacy, and to mechanise and impersonalise decisions on access to information, credit, and status, is the mainspring of a new collection of essays, *Resisting the Virtual Life,* edited by Iain Boal and James Brook. Many of the arguments are familiar, but still valid, and often well stated with new examples. I particularly liked the story of the Winchester house, built by the widow of the inventor of the repeating rifle, and so a permanent building site, deliberately never finished so as not to provide a roosting place for the spirits of Indians killed by the gun. Appropriately enough, it is about the only historic building in what is now Silicon Valley, home to the endless upgrading of computer programs.

The contributions to the book are divided into themes: "The New Information Enclosures", "Rewiring the Body", "Degrading Work", and "The Repainting of Modem Life", the last section being the most interesting, even if it fails to match the Baudelaireian implications of its boldly borrowed title. Covering subjects from the involvement of Gore, pére et fils in highways and infobahns, to the Microsoft Gallery as an arcade game, the screen saver as an icon of office boredom to the non-value of depersonalised information, the book offers a range of different critical perspectives on the role of the computer in the home, office, workplace and school.

While the book never quite comes to grips with the inherent anarchy of the Internet, which uses its open-access structure to cut across the themes of control implicit in some other electronic technologies, the questions book poses about the definitions of virtuality, humanity and society in an increasingly mediated age deserve everyone's attention. This book, and in particular the contributions by the editors, not only offers a valuable, if occasionally over-ideological, counter to the current euphoria for the information revolution) but also develops new lines of arguments about how we should see ourselves in the electronic mirror.

The Show Goes On

DIRK MEYERHOFER
MOBILE STAGES
avedition, Stuttgart, 1999

Niche publishing is nothing new, but has been given a new impetus by new technologies. I mean this in two senses: new technologies such as mobile telephony, web design and information technology have created new specialized readerships, on the one hand, and on the other, DPT programs, office scanners and disc to plate conversion have reduced the upfront costs of traditionally marginal publications. But niche is not the same as narrow: an astuter publisher today can use the committed base of a dedicated readership to extend understanding of a topic across a range of disciplines. This in itself reflects the disappearance of traditional boundaries to design or other creative activities which is a feature of the late twentieth century mode of communication.

An elegant example of the benefits of this tendency is Dirk Meyhofer's *Mobile Stages*. The book brings together a number of temporary architectural solutions, for trade presentations, exhibitions, musicals, circuses, pop music events, or open-air opera. The launch tour of the A series Mercedes, a lakeside production of *Nabucco*, a traditional big-top circus or the Rolling Stones Bridges to Babylon tour all thus fall under the same rubric as the Millennium Dome in Greenwich.

The images are stunning, be they of Hans Dieter Schaal's production of the *Magic Flute* in an angled, evolving birdbox, U2's pastiche Popmart by Mark Fisher or Hans Schavernoch's flaming highway for *Porgy and Bess*. What gives this barrage of stupendous special effects a degree of sense in Meyhofer's identification of three key common elements. The first is a certain shared cultural tradition, the second a perception of the nature of the design or architectural opportunity they represent and the third the synthesis between different media which they embody. This subtle understanding justifies his claim (and so validates the book) that such highly visual, complex, temporary, multimedia events represent a summum of many contemporary tendencies in architecture and design and that through them we can understand wider issues of presence and insubstantiality in conventional architecture, as well as the nexus between immediate and permanent, between perceived and seen, between event and fact, that sits at the base of many contemporary concerns about the value of the real.

As to the first of these elements, Meyhofer cites the mediaeval strolling players' cart-cum-backdrop, an image given a permanent modern resonance through Bergman's *Seventh Seal* and Stoppard's *Rosencrantz & Guildenstern are dead*. As a more modern example he cites Schinkel's work as an architect, urbanist and set designer, itself a continuation of the role or architect as metteur en scene embodied by Inigo Jones work on Jacobean royal masques. Another link could be built between modern events and traditional rituals such as the fiery dragons of Chinese New Year or Diwali in India where burning temporary structures plays a central part in the rite.

Meyhofer's second element is more important, for he makes the point that the invitation to build a temporary structure frees the designer's creative spirit from constraints (and indeed creates an echo of the kind of projects set to students, of creating immediate, blue-sky ideas). The possibility of constructing such unconstrained building is a wholly twentieth century one, born of the technological advances in materials and techniques the century has achieved. Not that earlier architects did not dream: rafts

of utopias drift down the historical stream between Boul-
lée's Memorial to Newton and Sant'Elia's Floating Cities
– or Archigram's Plug-In possibilities. But today an architect such as Jean Nouvel can not only talk about something as exotic as 'mono-matiére-mutable', but propose to
build in it as well.

Often these temporary structures combine different technologies for the spectacle they encase: lighting, whether
conventional or laser, film and video projectors, sound systems, mobile elements such as platforms, fireworks and live
actors. These are often 'cutting edge' technologies, but the
real technical mastery is to be found in the control systems that allow the complexities of simultaneous events
across a range of different technologies to be mastered and
synchronised into the total display. There is an argument
that control technologies are the real discoveries of the
twentieth century, and that industrial success depends today not on manpower and materials, but on the ability to
manage complex processes rapidly, efficiently and safely.
Certainly some of the events described here, such as the
pyrotechnics of the launch event for the A Class Mercedes,
depend for their effect on meticulous planning and split-
second execution. Compare this to virtual reality or even
sophisticated consumer games: they are only pushing pix-
els about, admittedly with speed and subtlety. The work
described here is real space, real time, real life.

Musical Scales

KIYOSHI FURUKAWA, MASAKI FUJIHATA, WOLFGANG STERN
SMALL FISH
CD-Rom & Booklet, ZMK, Karlsruhe, 1999

Take one composer, one graphic artist and one programmer, and what do you get? Small Fish is the answer. One
such small fish is called Honk. Click on the Japanese characters on the opening screen, and an outline figure appears, kicking a red ball. As the ball bounces around the
screen, hitting various boxes and obstacles en route, a series
of musical sounds is produced. The listener/viewer/user can
move the boxes and obstacles around, and change the on-
screen figure as well. These changes in turn impact on the
music. The images are flat patches of colour, but the sound
depth makes them seem more realistic. Honk is one of 15
scenarios or games on the Small Fish CD-Rom, designed
by the composer Kiyoshi Furukawa, the artist Masaki Fujihata, and the programmer Wolfgang Stern. It is published
by ZKM, a computer, music and art workshop and re-
source centre in Karlsruhe, Germany, while the two Japanese
authors were there as composer and artist in residence re-
spectively. Each of the games uses a similar arrangement
of moveable graphic elements on screen to create patterns
of light and sound that can be modified by the user/

So far, Small Fish fits into a long line of experiments to
link sound, light and colour that date back to nineteenth
century colour harmoniums and continue today with the
light storms built around rock concerts. And even is Small
Fish isn't as much of a blast as Pink Floyd's *The Wall*, it
does in fact take the concept a considerable way further.
As Wolfgang Munch explains, the graphic elements are not
simple symbols but objects, independent unities of code

that exchange information with other objects in the program, modifying them and being modified by them in the
process, according to the algorithms and instructions embedded in each object. The system or overall program contains and governs these interactions, without having total
knowledge of them.

This produces the delightful paradox that the 'works' produced by the program are neither predictable nor wholly
random, nor are they completely controlled by the user either. If you leave the program to run on its own for a
while it will not fall into a closed loop but continue to
evolve according to its own rules, one of which is, of
course, that the player may intervene at any time. So no
two runs of the same game are the same, although the
potential number of combinations is not infinite either,
since as Munch points out, computers only know one and
zero and so cannot know infinity.

Kiyoshi Furukawa's musical work regularly uses a human
player/computer interface as its locus, with the computer
analysing the sounds of a voice or instrument and replac-
ing or overlaying them with pre-recorded or randomly gen-
erated sounds (as in his 1993 piece Swim Swan). Often
these are accompanied by graphic images, as in the 1997
multi-media opera To the Unborn Gods, in which the mu-
sicians were represented onscreen by interactive graphic figures designed by Robert Darroll.

The artist Masaki Fujihata has his workshop and labora-
tory at the Shunan Fujisana campus of Keio University,
where Jun Munai, pioneer of WIDE (the Widely Integrated Distributed Network) that was so influential in launch-
ing the creative use of the Internet in Japan, also works.
Fujihata's art also involves transposition as a key element.
For example his Impressing Velocity piece integrated global positioning data and mapping images acquired on a climb
of Mount Fuji with the speed of the climb, so distorting
the image according to the climber's rate of movement.

And since the data sets that underlie his works are digital, they can be output in different ways: as stereolithographical sculptures, as video renderings, as prints or as online graphics. Fujihata often describes his works as journeys, where both path and map are continuously created and recorded as the work progresses: 'perhaps what I feel is the map chiding me for missing these opportunities. At every juncture a crowd of chances – each suggesting absolutely unknown worlds – lies at my feet'.

This collaboration between two artists and a programmer has not only produced an enjoyable and exciting result, both to see and hear. Small Fish also shows how the concept of multimedia can be extended through the conventional simultaneity of image, sound and onscreen response into something far more challenging and creative. The simplicity of the imagery belies the actual complexities that underlie it: the title 'Small Fish' comes from the habit of certain species of fish, when young, to swim together in groups that from a distance could be taken for one big fish, so deterring predators. But small fish grow into big ones: so perhaps these Small Fish will also evolve into new multi-media species.

Wine bottle by Starck for Good Goods, 1998

Designers at Work
and some sort of conclusion

Non for non

PHILIPPE STARCK
GOOD GOODS
La Redoute, Paris, 1998

"This is really quite simple," the designer explains, "non-products for nonconsumers in the future moral market." This collection of non-sequiturs is available as a catalogue, as well; probably it's the first time mail order has been used to announce the end of consumerism. But then the designer involved is the French design wizard Philippe Starck, from whom the unusual and provocative has become the expected: but what is *Good Goods* – his first venture into packaging design, his first into clothing, his first into food and drink – in fact about?

From the *Good Goods* catalogue you can order a motorbike or a push scooter, a gas-mask or a table lamp, a bottle of champagne or a packet of washing powder (both organic), a babygrow or a political Tshirt, an oyster knife or a fly-swatter, a cocktail dress or a canoe, a music CD or a packet of rice cakes, a pillow or a pullover. But the operative word is not 'or' but 'and'. Good Goods is a lifestyle catalogue: not Starck's remix of his favourite things, but a complete political and design statement. 'A collection of objects that are honest, responsible and respectful to people, for the citizen of tomorrow', in his own words, 'a vast, pretentious and naïve programme!'

The story is simple: approached by French mail order giants La Redoute for an exclusive catalogue of his own products, Starck decided to take their idea a few steps further in his own direction. He had already worked mailorder before: with La Redoute's main competitor, Les Trois Suisses in the 1980s for individual pieces of furniture, and later in 1994 when he offered a complete holi-day house kit (plans, instructional video, and free hammer) for £500. The aim was not just to offer buyers a model but both to show up the inadequacies of planning law, and the poor quality of the other 'kit' homes available on the market (which is why the Breton cottage and the Al-pine chalet have been found so often so far from their na-tive habitats). What Starck realised was that mailorder could not only present products but positions and ideas as well. This fitted with his growing conviction that a design-er not only has a positive social duty but that further that duty must be expressed through his work. And that the need is urgent, as he sees it, because a central concept is in danger: love. 'Love is what defines us as human, as a society, as a civilisation: without it we will cease to be human, arbitrary as a mental construct the idea of love may be... What we must recognise about being human is that it is a poetic concept, whose principal defining factor is love. Love in the sense of maternal love, which in turn originates from a shared desire to protect and nurture the species'. Starck's proposition is neither a scientific discourse nor a philosophical treatise, rather a basis for action. He is an autodidact, but he endorses the scientific method of proceeding by thorough and impartial analysis ('I'm a functionalist, not a poet', he remarks).

'The other key aspect of humankind', Starck continues,' is that as a species, as a society, as a civilisation, we are endlessly and continuously in a state of mutation. We have to accept that: so we cannot stand still and hope change will stop. It is impossible for change to stop. The main change in the last twenty centuries of human history has been humankind's power over matter, and the relentless search for material goods. With the invention of mechani-sation at the beginning of the twentieth century this race for material power has been faster and even faster, and always at the expense of love'. How can a designer inter-vene in this situation? Only, in Starck's view, by design. For example, having decided some years ago to give up

eating meat – an idea whose reasoning he has since discussed frequently in lecture and interviews – Starck then
decided to give the cause of organic and vegetarian food
a positive push, not just his support. He spoke to the
Belgian company, Lima, about ways in which to create a
new product line with his endorsement and so a potential
appeal beyond what he sees as the closed ranks of existing vegetarians. 'So an alternative tactic is to appeal to
people's personal interest: eat organically and you will feel
better and live longer. That, they are able to accept, even
if only out of egotism'.

The OAO products were ideal candidates for the Good
Goods project, and for the graphic design for the OAO
range, and packaging for Good Goods, Starck invited the
Swedish designer Patrick Granquist to join his team. 'We
wanted to make a very simple and direct statement', he
explains, 'in which the quality of what was on offer was
paramount: "what you see is what you get." It was deliberately minimal and open'. For the box packaging plain

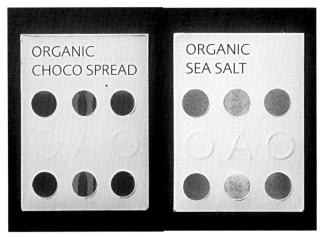

Two products from the OAO range

white card printed in black sanserif capitals, with the OAO logo in relief, uncoloured, and also, where possible, for example on boxes of rice or pasta, a pattern of holes to make the contents visible. The same theme was used on labels for bottles (organic champagne, wines and olive oils, for example) with coloured panels containing descriptive information, printed in silver script. This touch of colour gives a slight edge of speciality to the overall packaging solution, and builds in variety. For the branded products in Good Goods (organic cleaning products from Ecover, cosmetics from Bioderma, vitamins and ginseng from Europ-Labo, the same colour ranges were used: white or grey substrates with the name Starck in sansserif capitals. Virgin supplied a range of music CD's with themed compilations selected by Starck: these are presented in aluminium boxes with the name and Virgin logo embossed on the lid.

Because of its didactic purpose, the catalogue itself, edited by Pierre Doze, is replete with texts describing the items on offer. 'Because you read a mailorder catalogue, at home, at your own speed', he explains, 'we could set out the arguments for the products. You'd never have time to consider that way in a shop. So the offer is very different'. For Starck, enabling people to choose is part of creating a moral market. The cover of the catalogue shows a bald, three-eyed woman with a thin, formal beard. 'I am calm, I see the invisible, I am curious, I use sparingly, I am wise', she declares. This enigmatic proposal has already hit the right note: quite apart from the commercial success of the catalogue, the cover image has already been taken up by a French magazine as the first icon of the 21st century.

Losing and finding

RACHEL LICHTENSTEIN
RODINSKY'S WHITECHAPEL
Design by Mark Diaper
Artangel, London 1999

The history of the Jewish people in the twentieth century is one of diaspora and shoah: dispersion and destruction. The treatment of the Jews in the 'final solution' has become not only the benchmark for earlier and later genocides – in Russia, Rwanda or Yugoslavia – as well as a permanent and necessary reminder of the realities of humankind's cruelty towards itself, but is also a benchmark of the progress or failure) of the twentieth century itself. And seen from that standpoint the twentieth century has nothing to be proud of.

But under the shadow of the Holocaust other Jewish narratives of this century become, perhaps, distorted, or their focus changed. (The concluding scenes of Spielberg's *Schindler's List*, set around Schindler's grave in Israel, were an attempt to resolve this in a film that remains, for all its qualities, a soft take on its main source. Thomas Kenneally's *Schindler's Ark* or on the dark complexities of the real story). In this context, take the enigmatic story of an individual Jew, and set it amid the historical vortex of London's East end, and the question of how to tell this tale becomes immediately complex.

London's East End, and Whitechapel in particular, is a palimpsest of diasporai: the Huguenot French in the 17th century, the Dutch and German Jews in the 18th, Eastern European Jews in the late nineteenth century, Irish fleeing famine as well and the Bangladeshis today. At the same time the East End of London housed the workforce for London's docks, and lodged seafarers from all over the world. The Jewish community in Whitechapel, at one time the most enduring element, has now all but disappeared, but as a result of a voluntary movements: success in business has enabled them to move to more comfortable areas, and the demand for property in the East end, thanks to yuppiedom and greed for space from the adjoining City, has seen the end of small Jewish businesses, in favour of Georgian gentility, loft-style. (One of the last landmarks was Blooms Restaurant, near the Whitechapel Gallery, probably the last restaurant in London where the waiters bought the food from the kitchen and sold it to the guests). But for once the loss of Whitechapel as a Jewish community was a voluntary diaspora, not from oppression but choice, but in a people sensible of the genius loci, an event that left a gap.

Add to this web of histories an individual's history, and the skein gets more and more complex. The individual is David Rodinsky, a reclusive, poor, Jewish autodidact, who disappeared from his room above the synagogue on Princelet Street in 1969, leaving his books and papers, and all his belongings, even unfinished food. These were in turn uncovered in 1980, untouched, The story of David Rodinsky's life, and the interlinked myth of his disappearance passionately reconstructed by Rachel Lichtenstein and Iain Sinclair, are ones of individual poignancy amid a wider change and loss, his disappearance an echo of the greater dispersion, his remains a mute witness of times literally lost.

Lichtenstein's quest took her in search of the person, leading her to explore the streets of Whitechapel and their history (she now works as a tour guide in the area): the search also became one for her own Jewish origins (her grandparents had had a clockmaking business in Whitechapel) and their meaning, through visits to Israel and to Poland (Rodinsky's own family had originally come from the

Polish/Ukrainian border): her quest is about origins, and
since her account of Rodinsky is focused through a view
of life in the shtetl, her conclusion has to be in saying
Kaddish, the Hebrew prayer for the dead, over his grave
and so completing the rite. For Sinclair the story of Rodinsky
is a fount of metaphor and an echo of the stories of the
East End itself, as well as of earlier myths about the significance of place and absence: he looks back to the Cable
Street protest against Mosley's Fascist, to the underworld
of Jack the Ripper, even to Perutz's Prague ghetto. Their
interleaved account – Lichtenstein trying to discover the
reality behind the story, and Sinclair creating its mythic
context – has just been published by Granta. In the summer of 1999 the Artangel Trust published 'Rodinsky's
Whitechapel', as part of Inner City, a project on language
and location. It celebrates, through text and images, a
Whitechapel in which, thanks to these two interpreters of
his story, Rodinsky has found a place, even if his place is
gone.

Rodinsky's Whitechapel is a small 80 page book designed
by Mark Diaper. It sits solid and sober in the hand, with
dark, fully-bled images alternating with clean serif text, occasionally heightened by red type. The material from which
it is built is Lichtenstein's own photographs and artworks,
and Sinclair's and her text, as well as newspaper cuttings,
comments and images from other sources. It is a gather-
ing of words and pictures that do not tell a story nor set
a scene (for all the narrative structure implied in the map
that forms the endpapers). Rather it marks a closure and
a start: the ending of the quest and the consequent need
to readapt the mythic map of Whitechapel to accommo-
date that event. Diaper achieves this difficult task with elegance and subtlety. It would have been all too easy to provide a 'pocket Rodinsky' – a summary of the story and
its 'conclusion', or to have treated Rodinsky's story as a
metaphor for contemporary Jewish history. But neither
approach would have been appropriate to a tale both com-
pleted and incomplete. Instead Diaper builds a new pal-

impsest, creating through the simple, balanced use to type and image a new level of knowledge. Thus it is possible to approach and read Diaper's work without knowing the complete story, and without having to know it.

As Gilles Deleuze has pointed out in respect of Proust's *Remembrance of Things Past*, 'Truth depends on a chance encounter with something which forces us to think and to seek out truth... It is precisely the sign that we encounter, and which in turn exerts this force on us. And it is the chance nature of the encounter which underwrites the necessity of our thinking... What does someone want when he says "I want the truth?" He only wants what he is forced into seeking, under the constraints of an encounter, and in relation to what that signifies. What he wants is to interpret, decipher, translate, discover the meaning of the sign'. And since the meaning of signs depends, Deleuze points out, on context not one a fixed code, the same encounter can create in different people different truths, none of which is necessarily more valid or 'true' than another, but each of which satisfies the context of the sign. The parallel narratives of Rodinsky's Room show how the encounter with Rodinsky's absence created different spheres of meaning (often interacting) for Lichtenstein and Sinclair. Diaper's quiet but powerful reworking of these signs and meanings into Rodinsky's Whitechapel preserves their integrity while clothing them in a new meaning.

Marking Time

JEREMY MYSERSON
NEWS AT TEN
HGV, London, 1998

It's a truism that a design without a brief is an impossible task. Impossible theoretically, since by almost any definition design is a problem-solving process, so there needs to be some problem (if not one posed by a client) to solve, and impossible practically because what would such a design be for. So when designers come to celebrate their own achievements, they find themselves in the odd position of being both designer and client

Pierre Vermier, founder of the London design group HGV, wanted to mark the firm's tenth birthday, but felt a catalogue of clients and awards not to be the right solution. Instead he worked together with the writer and critic Jeremy Myserson, and the firm's designers, to identify ten global or national events from each year of the previous decade, and create a visual comment on each. For the fall of the Berlin Wall, for example, in 1989, a warning sign showing a demolition ball and the word Achtung, or for the opening of the Tate Gallery in Liverpool, a Henry Moore sculpture draped with a Liverpool Football Club supporters scarf.

As Myserson says in a brief introduction 'HGV's aim was to bring intelligence, wit and freshness of ideas to the fields of identity and communication'. From the work in this simple but engaging book, it looks like they are still doing so, and setting a modest example to their fellow designers about how to celebrate in style.

Count culture, not calories

ANNE MCCROSSAN (ED).
THE ENTERPRISE IG COOKBOOK
Privately printed, London, 1998

'First catch your chicken' Mrs Beeton is supposed to have
said: Janekë Rickard goes one better: 'First wake up your
scuba diver'. Then repair to the beach and hope there's
something for the barbie at the end of the day. This in-
struction is to be found in a book of recipes, put together by Anne McCrossan and others at the London brand
consultancy Enterprise IG. It includes recipes from the chairman and founder, Terry Tyrrell (fish fingers, marmalade
and Grand Marnier), the designer Rob Soar (his recipe for
Chocolate Oblivion includes a subscription to a gym) and
the head of the Knowledge Centre (an emergency mixture
of Weetabix, margarine and choking).

There is rather more cream, alcohol and chocolate in these
recipes than a dietician would recommend: this is food for
friendship, comfort, or celebration ('have a vodka or something and a cuddle with someone nice' suggests Anne
McCrossan, while waiting for her paella to cook). But it
is all great fun: detailed instructions on making toast, a
defence of the traditional artery-blocking English breakfast,
a carefully-crafted traditional Italian risotto, a Maryland
Cookie dessert (flight to Maryland not included), dressed
up with wit and illustrated with cartoon drawings and illustrations that make puns on the company's whorl logo.
Enough copies were set in Rotis (the corporate typeface),
laser-printed, French-folded and ring-bound, to provide a
copy for each of the contributors. The project happened
after Anne McCrossan sent an email to everyone in the
company asking for contributions. About fifty replied (out
of a staff of ninety) despite the pre-Christmas rush.

Festive spirit spilling over onto paper parody? There is, after all, a splendid imitation of Enterprise IG's prized brand alignment ethos, termed 'food alignment', on the opening pages. No, more an expression of corporate zeal, Anne McCrossan explains, or rather an outburst of team spirit. 'If our main business is branding and the system of values and behaviour that a brand implies', she explains, 'then what values and behaviours does the Enterprise IG brand itself imply? What is the culture of Enterprise IG?' Taking the idea of sharing food (or food ideas) as a ele-ment of culture and communication, she tried to see what degree of openness and response a recipe book could cre-ate. 'It's a measure of our sense of teamwork that we got replies, at a very busy time, from over half the people in the company. It reflects the spirit of the company and the commitment of the people who make it. The book is a statement of culture, and, I believe, to be successful a brand is also a cultural idea in that it expresses an organisation's personality'.

The recipe book was a spontaneous initiative (had it been a programmed project it would probably have been much more formal and much less fun). It has nothing in com-mon with the high-budget, high-profile projects that occupies the company's working time. And also it has eve-rything in common. A group that cannot reply with enthusiasm and verve to an extracurricular event like the recipe book is unlikely to bring a shared sense of purpose and energy to bear on its mainstream work. And not un-derstand the cultural approach to design and branding that is at the heart of Enterprise IG's ethos.

By way of Signing Off

GILLES DELEUZE:
PROUST ET LES SIGNES
Presses Universitaires de France, Paris, 1964

Neulise is a pleasant village in the middle of France. The
Route Nationale 82, until recently, ran through the middle of it, and the municipality, in a fit of civic enthusiasm
built a public convenience on the square in the centre of
the village. This modest 'aedicule sanitaire' is surmounted
by a metal and neon sign in blue and green depicting a
fountain and illuminated at night. Whether the late night
truck drivers or the daytime Belgian and Dutch tourists
following the lower part of the Loire valley were able to
decipher this emblem of relief as they passed I do not
know. As an exercise in the decipherment of a passing sign
it represents both an intellectual challenge and the assertion of a certain French vision of the world, by which the
subtleties of semantics are within the reach of all.

The allusive use of the fountain as a referent for passing
water would probably amuse Gilles Deleuze, a major contemporary French philosopher and semanticist. His book
on the role of signs in Proust's *La Recherche du Temps
Perdu* was published in 1982. Central to his reading of
Proust is his assertion that the work is not about memory
and recollection. but about what he terms 'l'apprentissage
des signes' By this he means firstly that the text of the
work is only understandable as a series (or more precisely
multiple and at times overlapping) series of signs – rather
than events – and that the author's purpose is not the rec-
reation of a forgotten and now remembered past but the
depiction of a learning process about the signs that both
indicate the past itself and enable it to be presented. The
task Proust set himself was not simply to recollect, but to

find a way of understanding the meanings and relevances of such recollections as he had. One way to do this – perhaps the only way – was to make memory into fiction, with time rather than the narrator the centre of that story. This device absolved the author from fact, so as to concentrate on the analysis and learning of signs and systems that in the end constitute the reality of his experience of time past, since the signs (rather than their referents) make the whole cohesive and meaningful.

Whether Deleuze's analysis is right or not in some historic or verifiable sense is not relevant, for as he points out for Proust himself the notion of truth is subsumed into the concept of understanding, so any definition of verity becomes a definition of standpoint, and so a semantic question before it can be – if ever – a real one. Deleuze also suggests that, whatever the fiction may suggest, Proust did not choose to write his great work: rather he was obliged to do so to exorcise the oppression of his memories. It is this quality that makes Proust's work, despite its historical setting, a completely modern one. Proust is, to borrow Northrop Frye's terms, the ironic victim of his own circumstances, just as Proust's hero is the victim of the sliding and changing patterns of the social and sexual world he finds himself in. Proust himself, and his hero, may appear to us snobbish and remote aesthetes, obsessed by appearance and style, as disconnected from reality. But they are so because of the compulsions of their situation, not necessarily from choice. We may not like them – but that is quite another matter.

I make this point, perhaps with a certain hubris, because a number of the authors whose books have been discussed here describe design and designers as if they were heroes and not victims, in other words without the ironic dimension which I believe is a fundamental aspect of the twentieth century experience, the ineluctable result of the experience of the First World War. This is not to absolve the designer from responsibility in any sense. Rather the contrary, the ironic character has as great an obligation to honesty and sincerity as any other. But to perceive the designer as operating outside society, or remote from society, or according to rules that only have reference to design, is to be in fundamental error. Design is important, and has become important, precisely because it offers, at its best, a set of tools for connecting with the world in better, more aware, more enjoyable ways. Design offers a way of measuring our situation, of interpreting the conflicting signs around us. To achieve that designers must think about the world, and the world needs to think about design. The world is changing towards complexity at a vicious rate: if we cannot use design to read the meanings of change, to encounter the opportunities and understand the risks for what Philppe Starck calls 'our mutating species in a mutating world', then design will have failed.

Index

Acknowledgements

The author and publisher would like to thank the following for permission to use illustrations in this book: Alessi, Agence Starck, NASA, Olivetti, Sony, Virtual Vision, Wolff Olins and Photos of the Great War at http://www.ukans.edu/~kansite/ww_one. Other illustrations come from the works reviewed.

Several of these reviews previously appeared in *Graphics International* and *World Architecture*, and I am grateful to the editors for permission to reproduce them here.

The idea for this book came to me some years ago, and so the errors, omissions and faults in the work are mine alone, but I would like to thank the following for their advice and help: Albrecht Bangert, Adam Biro, Gill & Iain Boal, Hans Brill, Chris Barrett, Ralph Caplan, Roger Conover, Siàn Cryer, Lucas Dietrich, Pierre Doze, Chris Foges, Patsy & James Fraser, David Godine, John Harris, John Heskett, Petra Kiediasch, Laurence King, Katherine MacInnes, Charles Miers, Jean Nouvel, Tom Porter, Tim Rich, Jocelyn Senior, Ian Shipley, John Latimer Smith, Nico Turner, Pierre Vermier, Solveig Williams, and especially Martin Pawley.